D1426968

014257600 7

24 HOURS IN ANCIENT EGYPT

24 HOURS IN ANCIENT EGYPT

A DAY IN THE LIFE OF THE PEOPLE WHO LIVED THERE

DONALD P. RYAN

Michael O'Mara Books Limited

First published in Great Britain in 2018 by
Michael O'Mara Books Limited
9 Lion Yard
Tremadoc Road
London SW4 7NQ

A CIP catalogue record for this book is available from
the British Library.

Papers used by Michael O'Mara Books Limited are natural,
recyclable products made from wood grown in sustainable forests. The
manufacturing processes conform to the environmental regulations of
the country of origin.

ISBN: 978-1-78243-911-0 in hardback print format
ISBN: 978-1-78243-955-4 in ebook format

1 3 5 7 9 10 8 6 4 2

Designed and typeset by Jade Wheaton

Printed and bound by CPI Group (UK) Ltd, Croydon, CR0 4YY

Follow us on Twitter @OMaraBooks

www.mombooks.com

In memory of Dorothy 'Dottie' Shelton,
who lived a life of joy and generosity.

Contents

INTRODUCTION

Of all the intriguing peoples of the ancient past, the Egyptians seem to hold a special allure for the modern world. Ruined monuments covered with a fascinating script, massive temples and pyramids, and incredible archaeological discoveries all add to the mystique surrounding a truly old and mostly vanished society.

Compared to ancient Greece and Rome, two of the other great civilizations of the ancient world, Egypt has not left us with a vast and diverse array of surviving texts that give us insights into almost anything that might interest us. The average Egyptian was illiterate and the majority of the surviving texts relate to things royal, religious and funerary. Still, enough bits and pieces have come down to us to allow Egyptologists to paint a reasonable portrait of its culture in its many facets, including a scattering of private letters and treatises about topics such as medicine. The practice of painting or sculpting scenes of daily life on the walls of the tombs of the elite – visions of an afterlife in a perfected version of the world they lived in while alive – have greatly benefited scholars. So, too, has the custom of equipping such tombs with actual food, clothing, furniture and other provisions.

A few abandoned villages have also survived. Although established in order to facilitate building projects such as the construction of pyramids and royal tombs, they were situated in arid places away from the Nile's banks and thus avoided obliteration by the cyclical flooding of the river. Excavations of these sites have offered us precious and valuable clues to help us understand ancient Egyptian ways of life.

The ancient Egyptians divided their day, measured from sunset to sunset, into twelve hours of the day and twelve hours of the night. (For the convenience of the reader, the modern convention of measuring a day as starting at midnight will be used.) In this book we will see what one of these days in the life of ancient Egypt was like, getting a glimpse into this vanished civilization through the eyes and experiences of twenty-four of its inhabitants, from the hard-working farmers, potters, weavers and soldiers at its core, to the divine ruler of Egypt himself with his complex entourage of bureaucrats. Each hour we will meet a different Egyptian, their lives, struggles and triumphs being of interest not only as vehicles for understanding what daily life might have been like for them, but also for what they can tell us about Egypt itself. Most of the characters and scenarios in each chapter are fictional but are underpinned by Egyptological knowledge, the intent being to provide slices of life in ancient Egypt in a realistic and, hopefully, entertaining fashion. A few, though, take their place in history including the ruler, Amenhotep II, his queen, Tiaa, and his vizier, Amenemopet.

The majority of Egyptians led relatively simple lives and loved their land, believing it to be the best place on earth. They called it Kemet, 'the Black Land,' referring to the rich fertile soil along the banks of its vital river, which snaked north from distant lands to the south, and ultimately emptied out into a great sea. The sinewy Nile Valley in the south and the broad Delta in the north provided a natural division of Kemet into two lands, Upper and Lower Egypt respectively, as they were clearly distinguished. At one time, the regions were politically separate, but their unification under a single ruler was considered to be the beginning of Egyptian civilization, and the ruler was well noted as the king of both lands.

The English word 'Egypt' is derived from the Greek word, *Aigyptos*, which seems to be derived from the ancient Egyptian word, *Hut-ka-Ptah*, meaning 'Mansion of the Ka (spirit) of Ptah'. The popular god, Ptah, was associated with the ancient capital of Memphis and was a patron of craftsmen.

The Nile River really was at the core of Egypt's existence. Its yearly period of flooding deposited rich, fertile silt that renewed the farmers' productive fields. Its water provided a highway north and south, lots of fish to eat, water for irrigation and plenty of mud to make bricks. Off to the edges was the Red Land, the land of desert and arid mountains – lots of sand and stone, a number of gold mines and the occasional oasis.

Other than the river, the most dominant part of the Egyptian world was the sun, that orange ball that provided heat and light, which descended into the west each evening to be reborn each and every day – or so it was fervently hoped. The sun was the god Re, traversing the sky in a boat loaded with other gods, or perhaps it was propelled by a giant cosmic dung beetle, or engaged in a slow flight with the invisible wings of a divine hawk. In the Egyptian mindset, all of these things could be true at the same time.

Although the sun was dominant in Egypt's physical world, the perceived presence of gods was everywhere – and they represented both the physical and the abstract. The gods numbered in the hundreds, with temples and shrines of various sizes peppering the landscape. They all had their start long before the beginnings of Egyptian civilization when a creator god, Atum, arose from a mound of slime emerging from the primordial waters of Nun. Atum, himself, proceeded to create pairs of other gods, male and female, who played major roles in the creation and maintenance of a new world. Geb and Nut were the land and the sky; Shu and Tefnut were air and moisture, and together they comprised the basic components of a liveable environment. Of supreme importance at the time this book is set was the god Amun-Re, who was honoured by temples proliferating on the east bank of the river, and who was given credit for much of Kemet's success.

Our twenty-four stories will take place in Thebes, a political and religious capital, during year twelve of the reign of Aakheperure Amenhotep (Amenhotep II), *c.* 1414 BC, during the Eighteenth Dynasty of the chronological period that scholars have named the New Kingdom (*c.* 1550 to 1069 BC). The New Kingdom was a time of Egypt's empire building, with its eastern influence reaching to the edge of Mesopotamia and its southern dominance deep into Nubia. It was a time of growing prosperity, with Egypt's rulers initiating both military and commercial foreign expeditions of impressive proportions. Amenhotep II bragged about his superior skills as an athlete and warrior, leading his troops into battle in a chariot pulled by brawny prancing horses. Back at home he was a great builder of temples, palaces and, of course, many monuments to himself. The New Kingdom was certainly an interesting time in human history, and arguably the apogee of Egypt's ancient civilization and, as the following chapters will show, an ideal era to serve as an introduction to ancient Egyptian culture. Let's take a trip back in time to Kemet and spend a day with the people who lived there.

7TH HOUR OF THE NIGHT
(00.00–01.00)

THE MIDWIFE
DELIVERS A BABY

May you die, he who comes out of the dark, who creeps in with his nose behind him, his head averted (so as not to be seen). May he fail at his task. May you die, she who comes out of the dark, who creeps in, her nose behind her, her head averted (so as not to be seen). May she fail at her task. Did you come to kiss this child? I will not let you kiss him. Have you come to silence him? I will not let you silence him! Have you come to harm him? I will not let you harm him! Have you come to take him? I will not let you take him from me! I have provided his protection against you!

MAGICAL SPELL FOR THE PROTECTION OF A BABY

Babies can come at any time of the day or night, and Weret has made Merit aware of this at least half a dozen times. Merit's labour pains had started while still daylight and now, hours into darkness, the moment of delivery is imminent. Weret, her aunt, who is serving the role of a midwife, is there to assist in the process, fervently coaching her patient and reciting incantations as Merit squats over several bricks in a room barely lit by a trio of oil lamps.

Along with her advice and spells, the midwife has brought along a couple of small statuettes, neither of which are, by anyone's standards, particularly attractive. The god Bes is absolutely hideous; nevertheless, he is there to help. Depicted as a short, pudgy, ugly dwarf, his tongue fully exposed and striking an obnoxious pose, he could, it is believed, ward off evil forces during pregnancy and childbirth. The other statuette, the fertility goddess Heqet, is represented as a frog and has similar powers, and is no doubt happy with the proceedings. She has been prominently displayed in the home ever since Merit intently desired to be pregnant yet again. Heqet's inclusion made a lot of sense: frogs do produce a great number of eggs and tadpoles, but they don't snore, as Merit's husband, Manu, is doing in the adjacent room after a hard day's fishing.

The rather ugly but strong and fierce god Bes was a favourite as a protector of Egyptian households. Squat, with a mix of human and lion-like features, he was thought to drive out evil spirits. Unlike much Egyptian art, he was often portrayed with his body fully facing forward, a posture that displays his frightening features to full effect.

THE GOD BES, A PROTECTOR OF THE HOUSEHOLD

Weret places both of the images in a position overlooking the birth to enhance their influence. Upon discovering that she was pregnant months previously, Merit had been given a necklace by her aunt featuring a string of blue amulets in the shape of Taweret. While Bes and Heqet are certainly unattractive, Taweret with her composite features is uglier still. With the general shape of a standing pregnant hippopotamus with the legs of a lion, and crocodilian features along her back, she is perhaps the fiercest of the three protective deities, with the ability, hopefully, of repelling any and all malicious forces. Though repulsive, the trio of deities are comforting to those they watched over.

With an outcome of debatable accuracy, the ancient Egyptians had a kind of pregnancy test: wheat and barley would be placed into a cloth pouch and the woman, suspecting a baby was on the way, would urinate on it every day. If the barley sprouted it would be a boy, if the wheat sprouted it would be a girl, and if both appeared, it was a positive but undetermined outcome. If nothing sprouted, there was no pregnancy.

With years of experience, Weret continues to coach while a head begins to emerge between Merit's thighs. She knows that there is no guarantee that the child will be born alive nor that Merit will ultimately survive the experience.

Within minutes, though, an Egyptian baby is born, its cries announcing its entry into the world. It is a boy and Weret knows that both Merit and her husband Manu will be relieved: the couple already have three girls. Although helpful with the never-ending daily chores, at some time those daughters will marry and depart to have their own households, leaving even more work for Merit.

But after just a few years, this new boy would be able to learn to fish with his father, which in turn would become his own career, and contribute to his family's well-being.

'Nefer,' mutters the baby's exhausted mother. 'Let's name him Nefer, the good or beautiful one.'

'Yet again,' thinks Weret as she passes the baby to its mother. There had already been two previous boys given that name but neither had survived more than a few months. Both were buried under the floor of their house. Perhaps this one would be different and would live many long and happy years, aided by several loving and helpful children of his own. And maybe those ugly protective gods would work their magic this time. 'Nefer,' the midwife says. 'It's a wonderful name but presumptuous – surely you're not expecting him to be both well behaved and attractive? Not likely when he smells of fish like his father! At least he won't be a brick-maker, I suppose.'

The average ancient Egyptian, if they survived birth and childhood, might live to be thirty to thirty-five years old. There were numerous ways to die including diseases, accidents during work, or fighting the enemy. Many relatively simple maladies, including numerous infections and illnesses that can be easily treated with modern medicine and vaccinations, could be absolutely fatal. Parasites and eye diseases, which could make one's life miserable, were not uncommon and evidence of various kinds of cancers is now being found in mummies.

Baby Nefer is arguably lucky to be born in Kemet, Weret thinks, what with its typically hospitable climate, and usual abundance of food, and a culture which provides, at least in theory, a tolerable life in the here and now, and one even better in the Afterlife. As an Egyptian, his culture is superior to those others who lived outside the land, including the Libyans to the west, Nubians to the south and Asiatics to the east – inferior peoples who could only elevate themselves to true humanity by becoming Egyptians themselves. Nefer didn't have a bad deal, all things considered, thinks Weret.

The baby boy will be nursed for a few years by his mother, and perhaps occasionally by a relative or wet-nurse, though Weret hopes she would be spared that – she is busy enough as it is. There will be a few years of playing and running about with other children, all naked with heads shaved but for a long lock of hair on one side. But all too soon, he'll be segued into his father's profession, doing minor tasks at first, but then growing more adept until able to participate fully. Time will fly quickly as it seems to do and there will likely be a marriage and children, and the cycle would no doubt continue unabated for eons. Yes, a predictable – and often tough – life is in store for this little one, Weret thinks to herself, watching the baby squirm in his mother's arms – she just hopes he survives to live it.

8TH HOUR OF THE NIGHT
(01.00–02.00)

THE RULER LIES AWAKE

He has trampled the tribesmen under his sandals. The Dwellers of the North bow before his power and all foreign lands fear him … the world is in his hands. Men are terrified of him, the gods are subject to his love, the one appointed by the god Amun himself … He has seized the whole of the Black Land, Upper and Lower Egypt being subject to his plans.

THE GREAT SPHINX STELE OF AMENHOTEP II

Amenhotep lies on his back on his ornate bed, his head supported by a rest of solid ebony, his eyes wide open, staring upward in a fit of tortuous insomnia, his body aching from the day's physical activities. Amenhotep, or Aakheperure as he is also known, holds the most vital and onerous job ever: maintaining order in the universe. It's called *maat* – a harmonious balance of truth and stability – and to prevent the world from falling into chaos, and as the divine ruler, Amenhotep is expected to keep the forces of evil at bay and please the numerous capricious Egyptian gods who could readily turn on his people at any time.

Being ruler of Egypt has its benefits, of course. Considered to be a living manifestation of the solar falcon god Horus, he could pretty much enjoy the best of everything, and do whatever he pleased, but there is a cost to it. As a god, day after day he faces the highest of expectations of his people. There were numerous construction projects to accomplish all over the land – many dedicated to himself – all the while finding ways to build, if not maintain, Egypt's considerable wealth, which is no easy task. After all, he had not only inherited his legendary father's empire, he is also, according to his many grandiose titles that are carved into stone on many monuments, 'the Mighty Bull: Sharp of Horns, Powerful of Splendour, King of Upper and Lower Egypt, Lord of the Two Lands, Horus of Gold, Son of Re, Lord of

Diadems, the Strong-Armed One, Likeness of Re, Son of Amun and Lord of All Foreign Lands'. He is the commander of Egypt's military forces and the high priest to all of the gods – daunting responsibilities indeed!

THE NAMES OF AAKHEPERURE AMENHOTEP (AMENHOTEP II)
WRITTEN IN HIEROGLYPHS AND ENCIRCLED IN CARTOUCHES

The rulers of Egypt had several names and titles and there were two names in particular by which they were generally known, inscribed within elongated ovals that Egyptologists call 'cartouches'. One is the birth name and the other is a name adopted upon becoming ruler. These two names conveniently serve modern scholars given that there were, for example, four rulers named Amenhotep and eleven named Rameses. The second name allows them to be distinguished one from another: modern scholars tend to identify them with a number, for example, Thutmose III and Amenhotep II.

Amenhotep is the seventh king in his family's line of rulers, a dynasty that began with the ouster of the foreigners known as the Hyksos several generations previously. From lands to the East, the Hyksos had ruled Egypt for about a hundred years until defeated by the humiliated Egyptians and chased from the land. The subsequent rulers of Egypt were not content to merely defend their borders, but aggressively conducted campaigns to subjugate, or at least terrify, their potential enemies on all sides. As a bonus to dominating foreigners, the fruits of empire-building have become obvious: lots of booty including livestock, captives and gold. And increasingly it is becoming clear that there are powers in the East who are themselves growing in strength, and who must be checked.

Amenhotep's father, Thutmose, set a high standard for any ruler. His expertise in plundering and subjugation are hard to match and even harder to maintain. Thutmose, the third ruler bearing that name in the present dynasty, had brought the Egyptian army far to the east, all the way to the distant Euphrates river, with a lot of battles along the way. His long career included seventeen foreign military campaigns, the details of which are proudly inscribed in the Theban temple Thutmose had greatly expanded. Thutmose's rise to the throne had been curious indeed.

Amenhotep's grandfather, the second Thutmose, had died after only about a dozen years of reign, the heir-apparent being a mere child. While still technically the ruler, the inherited role of the third Thutmose had been essentially usurped by his stepmother, Hatshepsut, who after a few years of acting behind the scenes, came out and declared herself ruler. Despite this unprecedented situation of a woman ruling Egypt, her reign was quite successful, with expeditions to exotic lands to the south and incredible building projects. With her death, the third Thutmose was more than ready to rule on his own and did so for over thirty years. Later on in his reign, though, he initiated an active campaign to erase the memory of Hatshepsut, defacing her name and likeness from her monuments and demolishing her statues. There had been rumours that this was payback for his being kept in the background as he had been technically the king during her entire reign. More likely, it was to expunge the precedence of a woman serving as ruler of Kemet. Egypt is a land of long-standing traditions, and the order is not to be upset.

Not surprisingly, Amenhotep's father hadn't talked much about Hatshepsut while he groomed his oldest son, Amenemhat, to succeed him. Sadly, the prince died, and Amenhotep was next in line. Thutmose, though, was able to mentor the future ruler as the two served as co-regents for a couple of years before Thutmose's own death, a death that transformed him into Osiris, the ruler of the underworld of the dead. Amenhotep in turn became the living manifestation of Horus, the son of Osiris.

The life of Thutmose III was dynamic like few others, and Amenhotep feels a nagging obligation to at least give the impression of approaching his achievements. He would need to live long and have much greater ambitions to come even close to matching the accomplishments of his father. The people expected success from their ruler; a demonstration of *maat* that gives them confidence in their world. Fortunately, Amenhotep is a superb athlete and while some might cynically consider his claims exaggerated, there is seemingly nothing beyond the abilities of their god-king.

Amenhotep rubs his aching shoulder. Maintaining a super-human reputation takes a physical toll and he occasionally questions his own divinity. Why should a god suffer such pains? The Egyptians see him as a great horseman, charioteer, rowing champion, runner and archer. They believe that he is capable of shooting arrows from a racing chariot through several thick ingots of copper, a feat recorded for the ages on a Theban temple wall. Surrounded by congratulating attendants, it's easy for Amenhotep to believe some of the grandiose hype.

Still, Amenhotep deeply feels the obligation to at least appear as powerful as his ingratiating titles proclaim him to be. Since becoming ruler twelve years previously, he has only conducted three foreign campaigns, his first initiated almost immediately after assuming the throne. With the news of Thutmose's death reaching the lands he had conquered, some of those under Egypt's dominance saw it as an opportunity to revolt, and their suppression was absolutely necessary in order to maintain and hopefully expand Egypt's hard-won empire. It was important to let

The Good God, Strong of Might, who is successful in the presence of his army; whose arrows never fail. When he shoots ingots of copper, he splits them like the stems of papyrus ... the strong arm of whose like has never existed ... The large copper slab at which his majesty shot was three fingers thick. The Great of Strength pierced it with his many arrows, all penetrating three palms and emerging behind the slab ... It was in the presence of the entire land that His Majesty performed this.

TEXT ACCOMPANYING A DEPICTION OF AMENHOTEP II
SHOOTING ARROWS AT A TARGET FROM A SPEEDING CHARIOT,
FROM THE THIRD PYLON IN THE KARNAK TEMPLE, THEBES

the foreign lands know that Egypt was still in control. Troublemakers needed to be suppressed, and those who remained loyal were rewarded.

After that first campaign came two more in years seven and nine of his reign. The fear of Kemet had once again been instilled in those who might consider rebellion. Dozens of cities and towns in Canaan and Syria had been raided and/or punished, and the booty acquired was truly impressive. Having a reputation as being particularly cruel certainly helped. As the supreme military commander, Amenhotep was on-site and directly involved, and his prowess on the battlefield, like his athletic achievements, were remarkable, at least as officially reported.

His majesty arrived at Memphis with a happy heart and as a mighty bull. The amount of this booty: 550 warriors of the Hurrian elite, 240 of their wives, 640 Canaanites, 232 children of the chieftains, 323 daughters of the chieftains, 270 concubines of the chieftains of all the foreign lands along with their adornments of silver, and gold on their arms. The Total: 2,214 captives, 820 horses, 730 chariots, including all their weapons of war.

THE MEMPHIS STELA OF AMENHOTEP II,
PROVIDING A RECORD OF THE SECOND FOREIGN CAMPAIGN

The tired king's mind continues to race. Another typically big day lies ahead. There would be meetings with his right-hand man, the vizier Amenemopet, who would report to him all of concern throughout the land of Egypt and beyond. There are building projects up and down the Nile, including the building of new temples and the maintenance of others. And there is the matter of planning for his own death with the construction of a tomb in the royal cemetery and a memorial temple where he will be worshipped for eons. His viceroy of Nubia, Usersatet, would be presenting plans and seeking authorization for various projects under his jurisdiction.

And, as is becoming routine, there would be a parade of visiting emissaries bringing tribute who would present

THE PROFILE OF AMENHOTEP II AS DEPICTED ON A TEMPLE WALL AT KARNAK

wonderfully valuable and interesting things from far off-lands. He especially likes these occasions and looks forward to the bowing and scraping of the colourfully dressed foreigners, a sure sign of his nation's continuing dominance.

Later he would dine with his wife, Tiaa, and enjoy the company of his several children. The food would be the best, as usual, as would be the wine. No desire would be withheld from the Powerful of Splendours.

Regular introspection is good, Amenhotep concludes, although doing so at such hours of the night is not preferred. Although he respects, to some extent, the simplicity of the lives of the hard-working average Egyptians who toiled daily in their repetitive tasks, he certainly revels in the fact that while alive he is one of a kind. Yes, ultimately, it's good to be the king!

After hours of restlessness, the ruler of Upper and Lower Egypt finally drifts off, but not for long. Loud screeching accompanied by barking and the scuffle of several feet across the floor of the sleeping chamber put an end to that. The startling crash that follows alerts a couple of guards who pull back the chamber's curtains and rush in with a couple of lit lamps. What was once a beautifully crafted calcite standing vase is now in pieces. Apparently one of Amenhotep's de-fanged pet baboons, which are occasionally allowed to roam the palace, is being chased by one of his hunting dogs. Both of the guards were appalled and apologetic, and when they attempted to clean up the mess, the king intervenes. 'Just leave it until after I get up tomorrow; I really need my sleep.' The guards backed off, while more screeching and the breaking of more things can be heard in the background.

'Some of my people make bricks all day and probably sleep better,' thinks Amenhotep, 'and there are probably few with misbehaving monkeys tormenting them at a late hour. But such is the life of the Strong Bull!'

9TH HOUR OF THE NIGHT
(02.00–03.00)

THE EMBALMER
WORKS LATE

It has been an extremely long day for Hapuneseb but fortunately there are only a few more tasks remaining. Recently there has been more work than usual. A spate of construction accidents and other unexpected deaths kept the bodies coming in and several are due for burial in the next few days. But with deadlines to meet and clients to please Hapuneseb can't afford to pack up and go home for the night just yet.

He reaches deep into an incision cut in the lower left abdomen of a male corpse lying supine on the low embalming table. With his arm inserted up to his elbow,

grasped in his hand, he jabs and slices.
owl,' he orders Mahu, one of several of his
present, who stretches for a large pottery vessel.
t close, I'm going to retrieve his intestines.' Reaching
again inside the corpse, Hapuneseb grabs a handful of guts, pulls out the slimy linear tubes and drops them into the bowl. 'Fill it with natron and bring me another.' This time, Hapuneseb would be going after the liver; then he would take on the stomach and finally the lungs. He wishes the incision were a little bigger. One of his colleagues had initiated the cut but then was chased out of the embalming house, where those passing by hurled both curses and stones at him. It is nothing personal; it's simply part of a ritual that rejects death and those who damaged a human body – which as everyone knows, should be inviolate. The embalmer who had made the slit would soon return and on occasion Hapuneseb himself would be forced to swiftly vacate the premises. It was an odd paradox of Hapuneseb's job that his work was both necessary and disdained.

Hapuneseb is a genuine expert at finding and cutting away the proper organs and retrieving them through such a small hole. The heart would be left in place – after all, it is the centre of one's being and intelligence – but all else had to go. The entrails would become a real foul, rotting issue if left in the body, but still, they needed to be preserved with much of the rest of the deceased. It is messy, nasty but necessary work.

←——————————————————————————→

The Egyptians saw the heart as the core of one's physical self, intelligence and emotion. Its pulsations could be felt while alive and stopped at death. Its pace could be felt reacting to everything from fear to romance. The brain, on the other hand, just seemed to be a space-filler in one's skull – it had no obvious function and no religious importance, though long before the time of Amenhotep II, doctors had figured out that fracturing the skull in different ways would produce different symptoms of unconsciousness and paralysis that could be crippling or fatal.

←——————————————————————————→

The bowls of entrails are set aside and when sufficiently desiccated they will be put in separate limestone jars, each with a lid carved in the likeness of the four sons of Horus: Duamutef for the stomach, Hapi for the lungs, Imsety for the liver and Qebehsenuef for the intestines. The jars, bearing texts noting the name of the deceased, will be interred in the tomb as separate but vital parts of the mummy.

Now it is time to remove the brain. 'Would you like to give it a try?' Hapuneseb asks Mahu. The assistant reaches for a couple of tools and approaches the head of the body. Inserting a piece of copper with a hook on its end into the nose of the deceased, he pounds through the fragile bones beyond until he reaches the soft substance behind. Swirling the hook around, he begins to break up the brain, liquefying it and pulling small chunks out through the nostrils. Hapuneseb watches Mahu as he eventually checks that he can now feel the hard walls of the skull in all directions and helps him to flip the body over. Mahu slaps it repeatedly on the back of the head to drain a ghastly substance into a pile of sand on the floor.

'Let's wash him out, pack him and dry him, and we'll be done with him for a while.' Hapuneseb shoves linen rags into the body through the incision and wipes it out as much as possible before putting the soiled cloths into a large white pot. He then rubs the body inside and out with oils and resins, and packs its void with some more rags, and inserts a few small ones in the nostrils. The incision in the side is closed with stitches and a small sheet of very thin gold. That being complete, the body is lifted on to a flat wooden tray in one corner of the room, where a large open jar awaits. Scoop after scoop of a white substance is removed from it and poured around, under and over the body until it is completely covered. This is natron, a product retrieved from a dry lakebed in the desert far to the northwest of Thebes. Its dehydrating properties are well known and essential for creating what is hoped to be a recognizable version of a once-living human. The normal process of mummification took seventy days, at which time the natron would be brushed away to reveal the end result.

Natron is a naturally occurring substance found in dry lake beds and is composed mostly of sodium carbonate and bicarbonate. A large quantity of it was required for each mummy and there must have been caravan after caravan of donkeys going in and out of the desert loaded down with the material to provide the vast amounts required in the embalming industry.

Hapuneseb is proud of his work. If a body arrives at his workshop shortly after death, he has a better chance of an excellent outcome and the work would be less odiferous. It is sad that no one other than the colleagues with whom he works can actually know the quality of his work. The preserved body would be wrapped in layers of linen and placed in a coffin for eternity. At least, that would be the plan. The body's life force, though, its *ka*, would have a home, and its soul, or *ba*, would be able to leave the body and its tomb to flit about in the outside world and return at will.

The origins of mummification are somewhat obscure although it's possible that the idea was derived from viewing naturally desiccated bodies. Simple graves revealed by shifting sand in dry desert areas could have inspired the idea that the same thing could be produced artificially at will in a relatively short amount of time by using dehydrating agents such as natron. Recent discoveries show that in at least one prehistoric cemetery, the practice of wrapping the bodies and applying resin had already been introduced.

←——————————————————————————→

Hapuneseb glances around the large room. There are several embalming trays mounded with natron covering bodies in various stages of dehydration. After the drying process the corpse would be cleaned and wrapped in a process less nasty, but still elaborate. The body would be wrapped in strips and sheets of linen with each limb bound separately. Usually, a priest would recite spells during this process, making sure that the dead person would not only be physically preserved, but would be regenerated as a transformed and immortal being. Wearing a mask representing the jackal-headed patron god of embalming, Anubis, the priest would oversee the wrapping process making sure that magical amulets were placed in the proper position on the mummy. A ceramic scarab beetle might inspire resurrection and little likenesses of the four sons of Horus might also be included.

A large scarab made of stone, its flat side engraved with funerary texts, is perhaps the most important amulet of them all. It would be placed over the area of the deceased's heart in the event anything happened to the actual organ left in the body. The heart is essential for the deceased's judgment in the Netherworld during which it would be weighed on a scale against the feather of *maat* representing truth and justice. If all is successful, a splendid eternity would follow. To finish off the mummy's creation, a mask with human features would be fitted like a helmet over the mummy's wrapped head, giving a human appearance to what might otherwise look like a tightly wound bundle of linen.

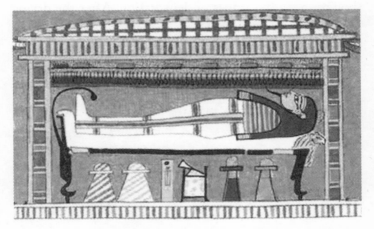

THE MUMMY OF THE SCRIBE, ANI, AWAITS TRANSPORT TO HIS TOMB, COMPLETE WITH HIS ENTRAILS IN JARS AND A WRITING KIT

It was very late, but one particular individual, Ipi, has his funeral in a few short hours and his body simply had to be finished. Ipi had been a particularly difficult case from the very beginning. A little over two months previously, he fell

The embalmers charge their syringes with cedar oil and therewith fill the belly of the dead man, making no cut, nor removing the intestines, but injecting it through his back-side orifice and checking it from returning; then they embalm the body for the appointed days; on the last day they let the oil which they poured in pass out again. It has so great power that it brings away the inner parts and intestines all dissolved; the flesh is eaten away by the natron and in the end nothing is left of the body but skin and bone.

HERODOTUS, *THE HISTORIES*, BOOK II, DESCRIBING ONE OF THE CHEAPER FORMS OF MUMMIFICATION AS IT WAS PRACTISED AROUND 450 BC

off the top of a wall and landed on his head. Apparently, he wasn't noticed (or was ignored) and lay dead for several days and some suggested he had been pushed. It wasn't too much of a surprise: Ipi was one of the most unpopular people in Thebes. A friend of a friend of a relative of the ruler, he had been placed as an overseer and was considered very abusive. The story being told was that he was atop the wall, looking for a good place to bark orders from and make his usual threats, but then 'tripped'. Ipi's bad attitude wasn't only reserved for the workers; he was rude and arrogant to nearly everyone he met, and most of his family didn't seem to care for him either. Still, he had a wife who must have tolerated him somewhat. If there were children, they weren't admitting it.

Ipi no doubt had plans for a long life and a pleasant demise. In the last several years he had commissioned a tomb, complete with a courtyard, burial shaft and chapel, in an elite cemetery on a hillside on the western side of the river, not that far from the embalming workshop where he now lay. His body had been a real mess when it was delivered to Hapuneseb, with decay well underway and many broken bones, including the skull. Still, Hapuneseb has seen worse, and when he started working on Ipi he used plenty of the more pleasantly aromatic treatments. The incense already burning had had to be doubled.

Ipi's wife, Baketamun, had appeared not long after the body's delivery, standing a bit away from the embalming facility. She hadn't seemed particularly distressed and wished to discuss the costs. Hapuneseb had outlined the options. There was a truly deluxe form of mummification that would be quite costly. Only the best materials would be used, the wrapping would be of superb quality and there would be plenty of amulets made from precious stones. The mask would be magnificent and gilded in gold. It hadn't taken long for Baketamun to decline. 'Anything cheaper?'

'Yes,' answered Hapuneseb, 'we could use less expensive materials all around, ceramic amulets and a well-painted mask.'

'Anything cheaper?'

Hapuneseb had been taken a bit aback. 'You could always take him away, drag him out into the desert and bury him in a hole if you'd like to be that stingy!' he had said, losing patience. 'How about this? We'll do a simple but unembellished job. You can bring linen from your home for the wrapping materials. We'll throw in a few amulets and the mask will be very average.'

'Fine. Go ahead. Ipi deserves nothing better,' Baketamun had replied, showing little emotion.

The embalmers are certainly ready to get rid of Ipi and fortunately on that night there are just a couple of final tasks to do: put on his final wrappings and install his mask. The contracted lector priest went home a few hours before but the work, nonetheless, still needs to be finished, so Hapuneseb calls Mahu over to join him. 'Here, put this on!' he orders. The heavy mask of Anubis is lifted on to Mahu's head; far too big, it engulfs his shoulders and almost traps him. 'I can't see!' exclaims the boy, the eye holes located in the mask's neck being way out of place.

'Just wear it for a few minutes. You've heard the spells hundreds of times. Recite them while I secure the arms.' Mahu's muffled mutterings are nearly incomprehensible while Hapuneseb uses up the last of the linen brought by Ipi's wife. A few quick wraps and ties and Ipi's mask is installed on his mummy. After Hapuneseb has helped Mahu remove the Anubis mask, the two considered their work. Given that it was a cheap job, the finished project isn't all that bad, although the boy starts giggling at the cheaply formed and painted mask. Baketamun probably won't care and, tired as they were, as the crew at the embalming workshop begin to walk home, they speculate about what sort of cheap coffin might arrive for Ipi in just a few short hours.

10TH HOUR OF THE NIGHT
(03.00–04.00)

THE OLD SOLDIER
DREAMS OF BATTLE

His majesty went forth in a chariot of electrum, arrayed in his weapons of war, like Horus the Smiter, Lord of Power; like Montu of Thebes; while his father, Amun, strengthened his arms.

Annals of Thutmose III, Karnak

It has been a rough week as the wretched Asiatic enemy put up a good fight. Although the Egyptian forces have suffered more than a few losses, it is nothing compared to their foe, who are now being killed in great numbers – that is, the ones who haven't turned and run. There are no archers or foot-soldiers better than the Egyptians. Merimose is one of the latter and he thrives on each deadly contact made with the swing of his battle axe or curved sword, and he especially loves the occasions where he can fight with an enemy combatant hand-to-hand on the ground. Despite a few close calls, the wrestling always ends in a dead opponent.

The charioteers with their handsome horses are the fiercest and most intimidating of the Egyptian forces. Fast and deadly, they can wreak havoc with their mobile archers. And at the front of them all is the mighty Aakheperure Amenhotep in his gold-gilded chariot, inspiring all to claim victory as the pile of severed hands grows higher by the hour. This is a great way of making an accurate tally of the dead, as long as only one hand is cut off each corpse.

Yes, it is a great day for Merimose as he stands over one of the fallen to search the body for anything of value before cutting off an appendage. With his concentration distracted, he isn't ready for what happens next. One of the battlefield 'dead' scrambles to his feet, flips Merimose over and slams him on his back, ready to deliver a fatal stab with his dagger.

Merimose wakes up with a start, his dream having been interrupted by his falling off the low brick bench that serves as his sleeping platform. It isn't the first time he has experienced battle in his sleep; it is a regular occurrence. Now well over sixty years of age, he had spent more than two decades as a soldier accompanying his king on battles that provided a wealth of exciting memories. The young boys and older men in the village all look up to him and with one eye remaining and several missing fingers, he is a survivor whose stories of military heroics keep his listeners spell-bound. There are lots of incredible anecdotes, many of them true, derived from adventures in the company of the previous ruler, the third Thutmose.

As a young man coming from a poor family with many children, Merimose's had been a typical path to the armed forces. He had been bored, unmarried and looking for something a little more stimulating than hoeing and harvesting. There was already plenty of help at home to tend the modest field so, to his father's relief, he joined the ranks of the army aged twenty. It would be one less mouth to feed. If he had been looking for adventure, he found more than he could possibly anticipate.

The third ruler with the name Thutmose had finally come to reign on his own upon the death of his stepmother and illegitimate 'co-regent', Hatshepsut. As was common in times of disruption or change, Egypt's subdued foreign enemies began to revolt and punitive measures were needed. Thutmose III immediately rose to the occasion and, mustering a huge army, he marched east to inform all that Egypt was still the dominant power in the region. Merimose was thrilled and got his first taste of battle, which created an insatiable desire for more. Thutmose wouldn't disappoint. During the next three decades, he organized almost a dozen and a half military campaigns.

That first journey to the east proved to be the most memorable for Merimose, who was awestruck at the size of the operation he was now a part of: the long line of soldiers bearing their weapons, the horses and chariots, and the trains of donkeys to support them all. Never having left the vicinity of Thebes during his life thus far, there was so much new and strange to see. The journey down the Nile on the troop ship heading north was fascinating: he passed temples and pyramids and realized for the first time just how big Kemet actually was. The march east, too, was full of new experiences and environments. Battle came all too soon and Merimose threw himself into it with youthful vigour and little appreciation for his own mortality. Stabbing, lopping, and clubbing … he had savoured it all! And now he did so alongside his new comrades as it proved surprisingly easy to subdue many of the smaller towns, while others required siege tactics to wear down the enemy trapped in their own walled cities. It was a lesson in the intricacies of warfare.

On that initial expedition, it was heard that a coalition of anti-Egyptian instigators led by the rulers of Kadesh was in the region, visiting the city of Megiddo. In a surprise move, the Egyptian forces were able to come up behind the enemy forces, causing them to discard their gear in a desperate attempt to seek safety behind the city's walls. In a rare instance of ill discipline, many of the Egyptian soldiers took advantage of the abandoned booty while many of the chiefs and soldiers of Megiddo escaped inside. (Merimose was proud that he'd resisted the temptation.) The Egyptians surrounded the city with a trench and a wall made from nearby trees to make sure that no one could escape. The enemy eventually surrendered after seven months of siege, which to a young Merimose seemed like an age – he was forced to learn his army's trademark patience and creativity. Ultimately, he discovered, this was the way to continued victories.

Success whet the appetite of both Thutmose and his forces, as those who returned home alive would be a bit wealthier as a result. Thutmose certainly would be, with a huge number of captives and booty heading west to Egypt – and so would Merimose. He and other veterans received small but very welcome land grants. Ever since the foreign rulers, the Hyksos, had been chased out of Egypt about seventy years previously, there have been military campaigns to the east, as well as south into Nubia, but there has been no one with the irrepressible energy of Thutmose III!

The humiliation of the Hyksos is not to be forgotten and it was somewhat ironic that some of the same technology that allowed them to dominate Egypt for a time was used against them by the Egyptians themselves, specifically the horse and chariot. It was a different and complicated kind of weapon, but very effective. The horses, most of which were imported from captured eastern lands, required special training as did the men who rode speedily behind them in wooden reinforced chariots. The charioteers were a special breed, and an elite complement to the infantry, and Merimose admired their skill and bravery. Two horses were required to pull the chariot holding its two occupants. One soldier was an expert archer and the other would drive the galloping steeds with reins in one hand while protecting himself and his partner with a shield in the other. At the battle of Megiddo, the Egyptians captured over 2000 horses and over 900 chariots.

The Egyptian army was highly organized with its ultimate commander being the ruler himself with one of his sons often in reality fulfilling those responsibilities. The army could be divided into northern and southern entities, each being directed by a hierarchy of officers. The actual troops were divided into a number of components including squads of 10 men, platoons of 50, companies of 500 and ultimately divisions of 5000. Of course, there would be a need for scribes for noting supplies, casualties and the accumulation of captives and booty. Additionally, a fleet of ships was available to transport men and equipment to convenient ports as needed, and also deliver the fruits of conquest back home.

Much of Merimose's training had been in hand-to-hand combat using sharp weapons. He had tried his hand at being an archer, but he just wasn't very good at it. Slashing and stabbing became his forte and in between expeditions he would train hard both in fighting skills and maintaining a high level of physical fitness. Still, there would be the occasional injury and Merimose had seen many of his fellow soldiers die brutally. He had lost an eye to a glancing spear, and then several fingers to the blade of an incredibly sharp sword during the same battle. A fellow soldier had stepped in and finished off the enemy combatant while an angry Merimose was pulled back behind the lines to be treated by a military physician. The soldiers were fortunate to receive the care that was available; Egyptian doctors were looked up to by people of other lands.

Despite the occasional setback, Merimose had enjoyed most of it, especially when returning home from Egypt to a joyous populace who lined the river banks or streets to offer their welcome. The pageantry was magnificent with grand ships sailing the Nile, and then on land where rows of infantry marched with their sharp spears and shields made of wood or cow hides, followed by archers with their bows and quivers. There were the standards held high, identifying each fighting unit, along with charioteers and their groomed prancing and snorting horses, and the field officers dressed in their finest. There was nothing like it.

Old Merimose especially likes to relate the story of

the conquest of Joppa along the coast of the Great Green (Mediterranean). The Egyptian general, Djehuty, negotiated with the chief of that city and offered two hundred baskets of food and other supplies. Little did they know that each of the baskets contained an Egyptian soldier who would emerge and open the city's gates to invasion. Being smaller than most, Merimose was chosen for this potentially deadly ruse, but it worked perfectly and the siege of Joppa was soon over.

But, feeling increasingly worn-out from years of fighting, Merimose retired from military life with mixed feelings at about age forty-five. He certainly misses the excitement of fighting in the company of his comrades with the charismatic ruler, Menkheperre Thutmose, leading the way. At the same time, he marvels at the fact that he had survived for so long, while many of the others did not. Fortunately, his extended family seemed to enjoy his company and make sure he is well cared for – and, after all, one of them would eventually inherit that land grant.

The present ruler, the second Amenhotep, is certainly developing a tough reputation, although the number of his military campaigns are thus far few compared to his father. As expected, the vile Asiatics began causing problems at the death of Thutmose so Amenhotep had needed to respond. During one successful rampage, he personally clubbed to death seven foreign chiefs whose bodies he hung upside down from the prow of his

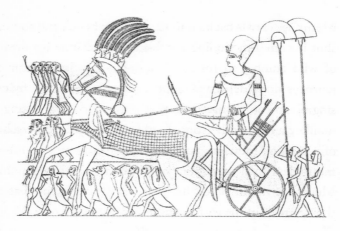

A NEW KINGDOM WARRIOR PHARAOH BATTLES HIS FOES

magnificent royal ship as he returned to Thebes. Six of the bodies were hung on the city's walls and the seventh rotting corpse was taken to Nubia and similarly exhibited to send a message that Egypt was both victorious and would not be threatened. The word has spread widely that the son of the third Thutmose is a force to be reckoned with.

The Egyptians had several gods that were patrons of war. The chief god, Amun-Re, could be invoked in vanquishing enemies as could Montu, a god of Thebes in the form of a falcon. The goddess Sekhmet, too, took the form of a lioness who was both protective and ruthlessly violent.

Merimose crawls back on to his sleeping bench and squints shut his one functioning eye, hoping to resume his dream of wild combat in foreign lands. His ensuing nocturnal journeys don't deliver as hoped; instead, there is a flying, singing crocodile snatching a basket of fish from an angry monkey, a fight with a long-dead friend over the ownership of a missing loincloth, and twenty dancing girls standing motionless in a sandstone quarry. And all through this, Merimose would fall off his bench three more times before the sun rises in the east to announce another day.

11TH HOUR OF THE NIGHT
(04.00–05.00)

THE PRIEST OF AMUN-RE IS AWAKENED

Hail to thee, Amun Re! lord of the thrones of the two lands
Thou who dwellest in the sanctuary of Karnak.
Bull of his mother, he who dwelleth in his fields,
Wide-ranging in the Land of the South.

HYMN TO AMUN-RE

Paser is sleeping soundly when he is rudely awakened by a kick to his side. 'Get up! Your turn is coming!' Paser glances around the room now dimly lit by a couple of oil lamps, a room where dozens of straw-filled mattresses lie about,

> *Handwritten note:* Sun and stars →astrology were observed in order to implement routine of attending to Gods

each cov   e!'
resumes   o
always k   w
much tin   r
most imp

They   f
Thebes. N   f
Egypt's s
elevated t
joined wit

well. The Karnak temple attests to it. It is already large and still growing, as are the property and wealth associated with it and the number of bureaucrats and full-time employees required to maintain it all.

The Karnak temple complex at Thebes is the largest religious structure in the world, covering over 100 hectares. Already established in the Middle Kingdom (*c.* 2050 to 1650 BC) the site was expanded greatly throughout the New Kingdom and continued to be enhanced thereafter over the next thousand years. Along with the great temple to Amun-Re, there were smaller temples and shrines dedicated to other gods and rulers, multiple sets of pylons, obelisks and halls full of soaring columns. It is truly sprawling.

Paser throws off his linen sheet and wraps a kilt around his waist and a shawl over his shoulders. It is time for the daily morning ritual. The god must be cleaned, clothed and fed at sunrise and there is lots of preparation to do. The group of priests gather outside of their barracks in the outer courtyard of the temple and proceed to march to the compound's sacred lake to purify themselves. Dressed similarly and bald, it is sometimes hard to tell one apart from the other in the flickering torch light other than by size and gait.

Reaching the lake, the priests leave their garments with awaiting attendants and enter the water, descending its stone steps until fully immersed. Every one of them is completely hairless, an aspect of purification that requires daily maintenance, and that is considered part of the job. Someone passes around a bowl of liquid from which all the priests sip and then spit. It is natron mixed with water. The god does not like bad breath.

As many times as he had done this, Paser has never got used to the often very cold water just after waking up. He always emerges extra-clean, he admits, and alert if not chilled. Drying themselves off, the priests are handed sparkling-clean garments and continue to prepare for the morning ritual.

Paser has been actively involved as a priest for several years. His father had been appointed by Amenhotep himself, and then Paser had inherited the honour. The priests were certainly needed. The ruler is technically the High Priest serving all of the gods, preserving their goodwill so *maat* would be maintained. But it would be physically impossible for him to be everywhere every day as needed, especially with dozens of small temples up and down the Nile and a growing number in Nubia. Apart from the chief gods of large important centres such as Thebes with its focus on Amun-Re, and Memphis with its devotion to Ptah, every district, it seems, has a special patron god.

If Amun-Re wasn't enough to keep Paser and his fellow priests occupied, the god's relatives, too, play roles in the bigger picture and demand worship. At Thebes, Amun-Re's wife, Mut, has a temple and a priesthood established for her. Their son Khonsu is also not to be neglected. It takes a great number of people and a lot of resources to support all of this. The temple of Amun-Re at Thebes owns vast tracts of land, much of it let out to tenant farmers who receive subsistence in return for their labour. Much of the rest of the grain or other produce goes to the temple granaries or storage areas where it is used to feed the thousands involved. There are huge herds of cattle as well, and a wide range of items acquired by donation, obligation or force.

← →

The priests at the various temples in Egypt were there to serve the gods. Unlike priests or rabbis found in Western societies, they did not serve as personal counsellors to parishioners.

Their job was to perform the proper rituals necessary to appease the gods in place of the ruler himself who served as the ultimate High Priest of them all, and not necessarily to facilitate the worship of average Egyptians.

←——————————————————————————→

To prepare the food for the gods and to maintain the priests and temple staff, there is a need for bread and beer-makers, butchers to process meat, weavers to produce fresh linen for the priests and washers to keep everything clean and pure, along with a host of other workers with other specialized tasks. Therefore, to supervise and keep track of all of these resources and temple employees, it is necessary to have a sizable bureaucracy – not surprisingly, there are numerous overseers, scribes and accountants involved.

Paser bears the title Fourth Priest of Amun-Re, which is certainly important, but not as much as that of the third, second and first. In time, perhaps he will work his way up through those other positions if they ever become available, probably when their occupant dies. It doesn't matter. Paser is doing his duty to Egypt's chief god and his title certainly impresses those outside the temple in his home town, a few days' travel up the Nile.

Like most of his fellow priests, Paser doesn't tend to Amun-Re full-time. At home, he is a professional scribe, and only serves the Theban temple three times a year, with each stint lasting a month. The system of having rotating priests diminishes the ability of the priesthood to become too powerful, and Paser thinks that makes his job much easier – it's better than being a full-time priest. He even looks forward to his duty each time, at least at first. It takes him away from his often routine job of recording tallies and he likes many of his temple colleagues, all of whom are educated, even if some of them snored in the barracks. As a literate member of the community with religious and ritual knowledge, between his months of temple service Paser often supplements his income as a scribe by providing ritual services to his neighbours, such as writing letters to someone's deceased relative whose intercession is urgently requested in some situation or other.

Now clean and awake, the priests walk through the still-dark central courtyard to one much smaller. This area is restricted to themselves or other necessary facilitators of the rituals, and as one progresses further into the compound, it becomes even more exclusive. Paser occasionally wonders how much the average Egyptian knows about what takes place in Amun-Re's temple. The temple compound itself is cordoned off from the rest of Thebes by an impressive enclosure wall, which serves as a sign to 'Keep out!'. Average individuals who have a reason to be there could come into the outer courtyard and take care of whatever business is required. One errand that brings people into the courtyard is to leave a small stela to thank the god for hearing their prayer. These small tablets generally have one or more ears represented on them. The visitors would see the many workers at their tasks, but access from thereon is usually restricted, with large pairs of broad tower-like pylons forming a gate to the sacred areas.

If they proceeded beyond, they would be dazzled by colourfully decorated columns supporting the roof. During the day light is provided by rectangular gaps in the walls near the ceiling. Along the way are walls covered with inscriptions noting the achievements of the likes of the third Thutmose and that of the present ruler, the second Amenhotep. There are the gleaming obelisks that all can see from miles away and side-chambers containing extraordinary items of wealth. In one room is the sacred barque: a small boat with a shrine aboard for transporting the image of the god during festivals. Each area constricts in size until a final chamber is reached: this is the sanctuary where the god is to be found.

A very faint glow in the east indicates that the morning ritual will be starting in just minutes.

THE GOD AMUN-RE

With the aid of the torches' flames Paser could see that the inner courts of the temple are sparklingly clean, as usual; this is the work of the *wab*-priests, the novices whose job it is to make sure that every place and thing is appropriately pure, including any item involved in the ritual. Laid on tables in front of the final chamber is an immense display of high-quality food and wine fit for a supreme god, a quantity of incense set in burners, a set of miniature clothing and jewellery, along with oil, cosmetics and pieces of fine linen.

Paser and the other priests lined up as the doors guarding the innermost sanctuary are unsealed and opened. Every phase of this activity is accompanied by the recitation of a solemn formula. Immediately the room is fumigated with incense and a lector priest begins to recite hymns to Amun-Re with the others joining in as a chorus:

> *Thy loveliness is in the southern sky,*
> *Thy sweetness in the northern sky.*
> *Thy beauties conquer hearts,*
> *Thy loveliness maketh arms to droop,*
> *Thy beautiful form maketh hands to fail;*
> *Hearts faint at the sight of thee.*

At the very back of the small chamber is a stone shrine; it, too, has sealed doors, which the First God's-Servant of Amun-Re steps through the torchlight to open, reciting the appropriate formula. As the doors swing back, an extraordinary image of the god is revealed: a stone statue with inlaid eyes, dressed like royalty and adorned with symbolic jewellery. The statue is only about half the size of a normal adult human, but the effect it has on Paser and the assembled priests is that of utter awe and due reverence.

The priests of Egypt did not worship the physical cult statue per se. They believed that a particular god was actually present and inhabited the image and thus could be addressed and praised directly in its sacred space.

The First God's-Servant performs most of the ritual. First, he needs to completely disrobe the image in order to prepare Amun-Re for cleaning. The clothing is put aside and the statue wiped down with new and purified linen before scented oil is applied. Cosmetics are added to the face and then fresh clothes are donned. In a fixed progression, a fresh garment of white cloth is followed by one of green cloth and then one of red cloth. Finally, an assortment of jewellery is brought forth and Amun-Re is supplied with a golden necklace and a crown, and last of all a robe of fine linen is reverently placed over the other garments as Paser and the priests outside continue their ingratiating chorus:

One and only one, maker of all that are,

From whose eyes mankind issued,

By whose mouth the gods were created,

*Who makest the herbage, and makest
to live the cattle, goats, swine and sheep ...*

He maketh the life of fishes in the river,

The fowl of the air,

Giving breath to that which is in the egg;

Making the offspring of the serpent to live;

Making to live therewith the flies,

*The creeping things, and the leaping things,
and the like.*

Making provision for the mice in their holes ...

Hail to thee, maker of all these!

One and only one, with many arms!

At night wakeful while all sleep

Seeking good for his flock.

The god is ready for the day, but still needs to be fed. Several trays of delectable food and jars of drink are put before Amun-Re while the chanting and singing continues. The First God's-Servant slowly backs away to leave the sanctuary, sweeping the floor to remove the footprints of any possible malign influences, then closing the doors and sealing them with a knotted cord and a ball of clay.

Amun-Re has been venerated, clothed and fed, at least for the morning.

Later, there will be at least two more visits to the image for noon and evening meals, and then the god will be locked into his shrine until the next morning. The cycle will continue, day after day, throughout Paser's month of service. On occasion, there are festivals in which Amun-Re will depart his sanctuary – with assistance, of course – and actually leave the temple compound. Despite its sometime mundane nature, Paser enjoys his service in the temple most of the time and there were some benefits. For example, he eats very well. The food piled up to impress and feed the god is distributed afterwards among the appreciative priests. The divine leftovers are the best in the land; perhaps only the king eats better.

In between the rituals there is much to do including shaving, with some of the other priests razoring the bits Paser cannot reach. The temple archives are available to research whatever subject might be of interest and, much to Paser's delight, there is often a lot of camaraderie and discussion among the priests themselves. This morning, Paser proposes the question, 'Is it wrong that I feel bad when I praise Amun-Re for creating creeping things like snakes, or flies, or mice in their holes? I don't like any of those! Snakes are dangerous, flies are annoying, and at home, the mice are constantly trying to invade my granary!' Most agree with Paser's feelings and it is good to know that

**PRIESTS CARRY A SACRED BARQUE WITH
THE IMAGE OF A GOD DURING A FESTIVAL**

he isn't alone, but the chanting and singing will continue as usual; after all, these are words established eons ago and Amun-Re, mighty god of Thebes, requires them to be spoken – praise for flies, snakes and mice included.

12TH HOUR OF THE NIGHT
(05.00–06.00)

THE FARMER STARTS
HIS DAY

As observed, these people obtain their harvests with less work than anyone else in the world, including the rest of the Egyptians; they have no need to operate ploughs or hoes, or to use any other of the usual means of cultivating their land; they merely wait for the river to on its own flood their fields; and then when the water has receded, each farmer sows his plot, employs pigs to tread in the seed, and then awaits the harvest. Pigs are also used for threshing and then the grain is stored.

HERODOTUS, *The Histories*, **BOOK II**

The sun is barely breaking on the eastern horizon when Henu wakes from his sleeping mat on the floor of his small house. Quietly shrugging off his linen sheet so as not to awake his sleeping family, he stands up, stretches and heads into the other room to prepare for work. He grabs a jug of beer from the corner and sloshes it down followed by a chunk of bread and a bite from an onion, before heading out the door. It is certainly a bit chilly but warmth will soon be on its way as Re arises in the east.

It will be another busy day, especially this time of year. After several months of flooding, the Nile has finally receded, and many of the surrounding fields are refreshed with the fertile silt deposited by the river; indeed, planting has already begun. Henu's plot of land is relatively easy to manage. It is leased from the priesthood of Amun, who expects that a certain amount of the yield – in this case, much of it – will end up in their granaries and storehouses. Still, there would be plenty to sustain his family with food for the entire year, along with a surplus to use for barter with those of other occupations.

For the most part, farming a large plot of emmer wheat and barley – the basic ingredients for the Egyptian staples of bread and beer – is relatively easy except for the sowing and harvesting. During the annual flood stage, the fields are always underwater for a few months, but as soon as the water recedes, there are boundaries to reset and irrigation canals to be repaired. The land might need tilling, or not, and that could involve some strenuous work by hand or the assistance of a couple of borrowed cattle.

The Egyptian calendar was composed of twelve months of thirty days each. An additional five days designated as birthdays of gods were added annually in an attempt to make up for the actual solar year, which we now understand as 365¼ days, thus the 'leap year' in the modern calendar. Being a society with agriculture as its foundation, the Egyptian year was split into three seasons of four months: flooding, growing and harvesting. Specific dates were tied to the year of a ruler's reign, for example Year 12, third month of harvest, day 17 during the reign of Aakheperure Amenhotep.

Today, Henu will need to break up the soil in just one small corner of his plot, which will require a lot of strength, before spreading the seed. Sure, he has a cow and a couple of goats, among a few other livestock, but the cow is being used for milk, and his goats wouldn't take a harness. Fortunately, his neighbour and best friend Seni is a herdsman and, in exchange for a basket of vegetables, two sturdy bulls will be lent for a few hours. Seni is already up and untethering the cattle, and the two are soon off to the nearby field. With the expertise acquired from a lifetime of labour, the cows are quickly yoked side by side and rigged with rope to pull a large wooden plough that will tear up the earth.

The ancient Egyptians during the New Kingdom had no coins or other form of monetary currency and the staples of bread and beer were a regular means of payment. Barter was normal and there was a unit of exchange called a *deben* based on a uniform amount of copper, about 90 grams worth. Prices of various goods could be assessed by their relative value in comparison to this measure.

Seeing to the affected areas would likely take them the next couple of hours, and sometimes it would be strenuous work. Even with Seni willing to guide the cows around, Henu would have to exert heavy downward force on the plough to keep it effective and on course. After that, the sowing would be easy. It would be just a matter of donning a purse full of seed and scattering it by hand followed by its trampling into the soil by sheep, pigs, donkeys or cattle. And for the seeds to grow it was a case of keeping the canals clean and functional. The grain that would sprout over the next few months required little care other than the occasional weeding, if need be, or the discouraging of vermin from the land and river.

The seeming ease of waiting for the harvest has encouraged a condescending viewpoint of farmers by some of the elite, who look upon agriculture as a somewhat lackadaisical profession, but that isn't really the case. Many of the farmers also grow certain foods all year round, including vegetables and fruit such as onions, cucumbers, melons, lettuce and grapes. Those plots are on raised ground and have to be watered and maintained constantly. In most cases, any ploughing here is done by hand, and water has to be repeatedly physically carried and distributed using large, heavy jars.

PREPARING THE LAND FOR PLANTING

Apart from wear and tear on a farmer's body, there are other hazards that lurked in the fields including snakes and scorpions. The cobra, in particular, is greatly feared, especially when the produce of the field is lush and tall. An encounter could go wrong very quickly, and a cobra's bite was more often than not fatal. Henu's own father had succumbed to the venom a dozen years before, despite the efforts of a local physician who tried every medicament and magical spell in his repertoire to no avail. There are other dangerous snakes such as the horned viper – best not to anger – but the cobra could also spit its poison from a short distance, aiming for the eyes and often causing blindness.

Scorpions, too, could be problematic. They could be found in dozens of unexpected places, under rocks and behind home furnishings, ready and willing to swing their stinger into a hand or foot. Although causing severe pain and feverish symptoms, scorpions rarely kill grown adults, but children certainly could succumb. Snakes and scorpions both could make their way into homes, preferring to stay hidden, but willing to react at a moment's disturbance.

As a feared, dangerous creature, the cobra was a powerful symbol in ancient Egypt. It was sometimes featured on the forehead of the royal headdress and represented the intimidating and commanding authority of the ruler, and the goddess who protected and defended him, who was identified with the eye of the sun-god himself.

Unable to grow grain when the river floods every year, most farmers are not just sitting around relaxing. They could be put to work at home or helping with other professions. And there is always the possibility that they would be recruited for national projects that required the assistance, if not brute strength, of thousands of men. Henu has heard of the mammoth artificial mountains far to the north – tombs of ancient rulers – that were built in such a way. With a wife, children and some vegetables to grow, he prefers to stay at home rather than being drafted to work elsewhere.

The ancient Egyptian literary work known as the *Satire of the Trades* warns young scribes-in-training of the horrors of many ordinary jobs including the agricultural professions, and the grape-grower is specifically cited: 'The vintner bears a yoke across his shoulders, and each shoulder is burdened with age. There is a swelling on his neck and it festers. He spends the morning watering leeks and the evening nurturing coriander after spending the middle of the day in the palm grove. More than any other profession he becomes exhausted and dies.'

Harvesting certainly is no joy. The stalks of grain are cut by hand and then threshed and winnowed. A quantity of loosened grain is deposited in a simple home granary annexed to the house but the majority is given to the landowners, the priesthood of Amun in Hanu's case, and they are certain to appear at some point with a scribe in tow. They would retrieve their share, and the straw from the grain stalks could be used for animal fodder or put to use by the brick-makers. Harvesting flax isn't particularly easy either. The plant requires some extensive processing before its fibres can be processed into cloth, but that's the weavers' problem.

Even when metal such as copper was available, the Egyptian farmers still often used wooden sickles fitted with serrated blades chipped from flint. This technology had been in use from the earliest days of agriculture and, although the wooden handles would rot away over time, the discovery of such imperishable stone sickle blades indicates to archaeologists that agriculture was being practised at an ancient site.

With Seni's assistance, Henu will likely have finished working on the area to be tended in another hour or so, then he'll tour the canals surrounding his property. If all is in order, he'll drop by his home for another few bites of food before loading up his donkey with a few hand tools and heading up to the vegetable garden later this morning. Henu feels he should also invite Seni round for dinner. Seni is unmarried and often sleeps near his herd in a crude hut made from branches. Henu has often invited him over, much to the disapproval of his wife, Mutemwia, who finds him dirty and boring in conversation. She says he often showed up reeking of excessive beer, and then drinks far more than his share as a guest. Maybe she has a point.

Henu knows that when he briefly returns home after

checking the irrigation he will find Mutemwia already busy making bread. Soon, she will start preparing food for the main meal in the evening, which in many cases is the highlight of Henu's day. Often it is a stew composed of vegetables from their own garden, spiced with salt and coriander, or maybe something that has been obtained by trading. Grilled fish is always a possibility. Manu the fisherman lives down the way and he almost always has something available on a good day.

Many of the elite tombs of Egypt's bureaucrats during the New Kingdom contain beautiful wall paintings depicting agricultural activities as part of a hoped-for utopian Afterlife. Interestingly, the well-heeled official/tomb-owner might even be seen ploughing a field in his best pleated linen skirt with his wife alongside, apparently to show how they facilitated a bountiful crop with ease. Scenes of offerings to the deceased would often feature tables loaded with agricultural goods and chunks of meat. In some cases, baskets of actual food items were put into the tomb for the mummy's sustenance.

On occasion, Henu would slaughter one of the sheep or pigs living in his house, especially when their numbers are increasing. The fat from the tail of a sheep is especially useful as it could be used for frying. The cow, however, is not to be touched. Its milk is put to use nearly every day. Beef is food for the wealthy and Henu and his family barely have it once a year, and then only at a special celebration such as a marriage banquet or even a funeral.

Henu pushes down hard on the plough as his friend leads the bulls. Even though he is a herder, none of the cattle supervised by Seni are his own. They, like the land Henu works, belong to the temple estate and he is paid with regular bread and beer rations. The work can be sporadically difficult, but most of it is just making sure his charges are well fed, watered and healthy. This could involve moving a dozen head from place to place, and then a lot of sitting. Seni has to be skilled, though, in a variety of tasks, including tending to minor wounds the animals might incur, breaking up altercations between annoyed beasts, and delivering and caring for newborn calves. In extreme cases, a veterinarian might be called in to deal with confounding injuries and diseases.

The Egyptians were concerned annually about the level of the Nile. If it was too high, it could cause devastation to villages. If it was too low, then the crop yield might be lessened and in a worse case, there would be famine. Devices to track water levels were constructed along the Nile, which scholars refer to as Nilometers, several of which still survive. Prayers could be used to appease to the Nile god, Hapi, who was usually depicted as a fat man with green skin and plants growing out of the top of his head.

For now the ploughing goes on, Seni guiding the bulls around the field as Henu churns the earth. The sun continues to traverse the sky on a course just as inevitable as that of any farmer's day in Kemet took. For them the work never stops.

1ST HOUR OF THE DAY
(06.00–07.00)

THE HOUSEWIFE
MAKES BREAD

A favour which the ruler gives to Osiris, the great god, that he might give offerings consisting of 1,000 loaves of bread, 1,000 jugs of beer, oxen and fowl, alabaster and clothing.

A TYPICAL OFFERING INSCRIPTION FOUND IN FUNERARY TEXTS

Mutemwia finally wakes up as sunrays enter the house. In the distance she can hear Seni the herder yelling something at a pair of bulls. 'Must you make so much noise?' thinks Mutemwia, distracting herself from having to get up. She has slept in but now gets up and considers her day. Milk the cow, feed the children and Henu's widowed mother, Katabet, make bread and beer, mend and wash clothing, tend to the animals, feed the family some more ... the chores are endless.

Looking around her small three-room home, she gives little consideration to the fact that apart from births, deaths and occasional celebrations and religious festivals, one day is pretty much the same as the next most of the time. When she awoke each morning, her husband typically would be already off to work, and her children would be soundly sleeping next to her while her mother-in-law snored nearby, loudly and incessantly.

Grabbing a milk jug, Mutemwia nearly trips over a couple of geese quacking in the front room, and then squints in the bright sunlight before finding the cow tethered near the door of the house. The cow barely notices, contently chewing fodder while the vessel is filled. Mutemwia goes inside and wakes her young children, serving each a bowl of mash composed of bread soaked in the fresh milk. Katabet, too, gets up and sits with the children while Mutemwia puts on a simple kilt coming up to her waist, all that would comprise her clothes for the day.

Mutemwia only has three children, two young boys under four years and a six-year-old girl, all too young to be of much help in the fields or in the house, although her daughter often follows her around and imitates her. Katabet, however, will supervise the children throughout the day so Mutemwia can go about her business. Nearly toothless and a bit feeble, Katabet's job is to keep them out of trouble and danger in the hope that they might survive childhood.

The home's supply of bread and beer is nearly exhausted and it is time to once again produce batches of these classic Egyptian staples. The agricultural blessings of the river almost guaranteed that no resident of Kemet would ever starve and, even when the Nile disappointed, granaries large and small usually hold a surplus. The fields are so productive that, on occasion, tribes from Libya or Canaan would drift into Lower Egypt to escape famine in their own lands.

The process of transforming grain from the field into flour could leave a certain amount of grit in Egyptian bread. Additional grit could be blown in by winds from the desert. It could take a certain toll on the consumer's teeth as evidenced by heavy wear found on many an excavated skull or mummy.

Mutemwia reaches into the small bricked granary built on to the side of the house and fills a basket with coarse grain, bringing it inside to where the grinding stone awaited. Taking a place on her knees, she throws handfuls of wheat on the quern. Leaning forward she pounds and rolls the grain with the round stone in an effort to pulverize it into flour. Back and forth, back and forth, emptying the flour into a shallow bowl before adding more wheat. With a sufficient quantity produced, she pours a little water into the bowl and the kneading process begins, with both hands mixing, grasping and twisting.

WINNOWING AND MEASURING WHEAT IN PREPARATION FOR BREAD-MAKING

Mutemwia has a couple of options for baking. Sometimes she fills a cone-shaped pottery mould with dough and build a fire under or around it. Alternatively, she has a small domed kiln that can be heated up; thin patties of dough can be slapped on its wall and then peeled off when sufficiently cooked. Mutemwia chooses the former and selects several moulds to be stuffed and added to the small fire built on a growing pile of ashes. From then, it will be just a matter of not over-baking it.

Bread was a normal part of temple offerings, sometimes in huge quantities. A record of a festival celebrating the god Amun-Re and the other gods of Thebes during the time of the New Kingdom pharaoh Rameses III notes 'fine bread' in the amount of 2,844,357 loaves.

Along with the bread there was the matter of beer, which apart from fetching clean water from the river, is relatively easy to make. Mutemwia stuffs a couple of chunks of barley bread into a couple of large jugs leaning against an inside wall and adds a few dates to each from the palms in Henu's garden; occasionally she uses honey when some is available. Finally, she scratches a mark on the jar's side to make it easily distinguishable from the water and what is left of the old beer.

Everyone drinks beer. It seems to take away some of the curious tastes found in river water and is arguably healthier. It couldn't be very strong lest it detract from one's work. Mutemwia is certainly aware of this and carefully monitors the fermentation process. When the beer is ready in a few days, it will be strained to remove the bits of slimy barley-bread residue and soggy dates. Still, if enough is consumed, it is possible to become very drunk. Seni is living proof of that.

Like beef, wine is mostly reserved for the wealthy or an occasional special celebration. Yet because Henu's garden contains a few grapes, Mutemwia has experimented a little with making some of her own. There didn't seem much to it: add the juice from squeezed grapes in a jug and wait. Her results weren't that good. It was too sweet and it made Katabet drunk and silly. Surely there is a better method. The professional vintners must certainly be experts – Mutemwia has seen plenty of ships arriving at the port of Thebes, unloading large quantities of the distinctive wine vessels, a far cry from her own efforts, judging by demand for the beverage. Many of the boats originated in Lower Egypt, she had been told, and others were imported from Canaan or other far-off foreign lands.

Bread made and beer started, there is still plenty more work to fill the day. Laundry is next. The children could tag along as long as they played a sufficient distance from the river bank. Kilts, skirts, shirts, dresses and loincloths are piled into a large basket, which Mutemwia balances on her head as she makes her way down to the Nile. Smooth stones washed to the water's edge could be used for scrubbing and pounding out the grime. Henu's clothes are often filthy from working in the fields and garden, but the children rarely dirty clothing as they are completely naked most of the time, although they have endless ways to make themselves covered with mud or dust.

The washing area is a good place for Mutemwia to hear all the local news while minding her task with the other women. There are political rumours, gossip, family updates and a lot of sharing of advice. As tedious as washing is, the social interaction with the other women of the village is the highlight of the day. The laundry will then be taken back to the house where it will be hung to dry in the sun.

When Mutemwia gets home she will instruct the children to grab tiny armloads of fodder. It will add little to the amount actually needed, but it is good training for when they become bigger and the entire task is assigned to them. Some bits of grain will be spread around for the ducks, while Mutemwia sweeps the inside floors of random residues. After the clothes have dried, several items will require mending, and Mutemwia will sit cross-legged on a mat near the door and sew the necessary repairs.

In Egyptian art, males were typically depicted with reddish skin while that of women was often yellowish in colour. The standard interpretation is that it is representative of the ancient division of labour in which men worked mostly outdoors and women mostly indoors. It is certain, though, that a lot of chores conducted by women brought them outside of the home and into the tanning rays of the sun.

There would be a light afternoon meal, which might consist of more bread, beer and some fruits and vegetables. Nice slices of melon and a raw onion could keep one satisfied until the evening repast. Tonight it would probably be a stew and grilled fish, a family favourite. Before that could happen, Mutemwia would have to walk to the river to exchange some bread for some Nile perch. Henu would be home just before dark and no doubt comment about how strenuous his day had been, mostly neglecting the fact that his wife's day allowed no free time whatsoever and most of her chores were patently unpleasant and often strenuous. But Henu does always arrive with a few sticks of wood or other burnable scraps to help keep the fire going, throwing it in a pile near the granary, so that is something, Mutemwia supposed.

Sadly, she suspects Seni will show up for dinner, probably drunk, given Henu has been working with him today, and ask immediately for some beer. He always talks incessantly on subjects of little interest, and without fail blurts out some unintentional insult against Mutemwia, Katabet or the children. And he will eat more than his fair share of food. Despite all of this, Henu seems to ignore it all. Periodically Seni will stumble out of the house to relieve himself in the street and eventually he wouldn't return. Only then can Mutemwia tidy up.

Life could sometimes be thankless, but such is the lot of a housewife in Egypt.

THE OVERSEER VISITS
THE QUARRY

*She made them as her monument for her father, the god
Amun, Lord of Thebes, Presider over Karnak, making for
him two great obelisks of enduring granite of the South,
their summits being of electrum of the best of every country,
which can be seen on both sides of the river. Their rays flood
the Two Lands when the sun rises between them, as he
dawns in the horizon of heaven.*

INSCRIPTION ON THE BASE OF AN OBELISK COMMISSIONED BY
THE FEMALE RULER, HATSHEPSUT, AT THE TEMPLE OF KARNAK

The walk to the quarry is hot; hot enough that even the strict overseer, Piay, is almost beginning to feel sorry for the workmen, but not quite. Even from a distance, the loud pounding of stone can be distinctly heard in various coordinated and random patterns. It is clear that several projects are in the works simultaneously. Situated outside the town of Sunu (Aswan) at Egypt's southern frontier, the quarry has been a favourite source for some of the best granite in Egypt, its highly desired reddish tinge being found long distances from the quarry in monuments all along the Nile dating back many centuries.

There is very little work in the quarry that isn't in some way strenuous, physically if not mentally taxing, or even occasionally frightening. Any time the moving of large stones is involved, injuries are always possible, and there have been plenty recently. A couple of men were recently killed when a large block unexpectedly cut loose, and another had a foot crushed while dragging a large stone out of the quarry aboard a sledge. And then there are the men who pass out in the heat or simply die from over-exertion. Then again, concludes Piay, most are foreign captives or Egyptian criminals. They deserve such labour, the latter for working against *maat*, the former for not being Egyptian. Many are Nubians, Aswan being situated not far from the frontier of their land.

Reaching the quarry, Piay sees dozens of barely clad men at work on various tasks including the processing of stone blocks of the appropriate size for the creation of a royal sculpture. When ready, they would be hauled to the river on wooden sledges pulled by dozens of men bearing ropes. Reaching the bank, the blocks would be carefully slid aboard a wide barge for transport downstream to Thebes. The sculptors there would shape them into impressive works. Piay has seen a great many examples, and even though he appreciates the difficulty of releasing granite from the quarry, he is more impressed by the art of carving delicate facial features or detailed hieroglyphs in the very hard stone.

The mission today is to inspect the progress of work on two obelisks ordered by the ruler. These tapering shafts, topped by a miniature pyramid, will represent not only the rays of the sun god Re, but Re himself, as he had manifested himself at the very beginning of creation. Piay's last visit was two months previously, the quarry being one of many he is responsible for. At least this one is near the water and not far out in the desert. The quarries in the eastern desert involve a lot of overland travel, with caravans providing support to the suffering workmen. And then once the stone blocks are cut, they have to be dragged on sledges for days to reach the river and their eventual destinations.

The reddish-hued granite of the quarry is highly prized, but very difficult to work. The usual method of freeing the blocks from the walls is to pound trenches behind them by means of balls made from dolerite, a stone much harder than granite. Each strike might release a few specks of

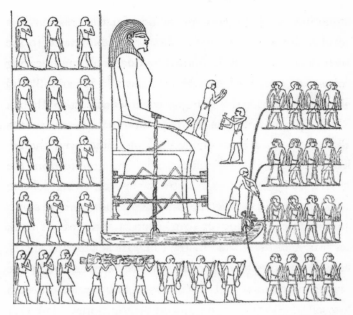

**WHETHER OBELISKS OR COLOSSAL STATUES, THE EGYPTIANS
WERE MASTERS AT STONEWORK AND SCULPTURE**

rock and, depending on the size of the block, it might take
dozens of men many days of constant bashing. Once the
sides have been channelled away from the mother rock, the
block can be freed by chipping away at the base. It is a scary
prospect but supports of stones placed beneath as the work
progresses would, hopefully, keep the workmen from being
crushed. Pulling with ropes or prying would finally bring
the block loose.

Compared to granite, which is so much more difficult
to work with, sandstone and limestone are relatively easy

to cut and shape. Metal saws could be used in the quarries and stone blocks could be procured in a matter of hours compared to the days often required with granite. And limestone is everywhere, although of varying quality. Many of the tombs of the elite were carved directly into the thick deposits found in the mountains of western Thebes, including the hidden cemetery of the rulers, a not so well-kept secret.

In terms of his building accomplishments, his king, Aakheperure Amenhotep, is far less ambitious than his predecessors. Amenhotep's step-grandmother, whose name is to be forgotten, was an active builder and at the Karnak temple she installed two pairs of soaring granite obelisks, the pyramidions at their apex encased in gleaming electrum. She also constructed an incredible memorial temple to herself along the cliffs of western Thebes, and although now much ignored, it proudly displays carved reliefs and descriptions of the cutting and transport of these monoliths. And Amenhotep's own father, Menkheperre Thutmose, commissioned three pairs of obelisks, standing tall and magnificent at the Theban temples to Amun.

While the works of Hatshepsut and Thutmose are numerous and obvious to all, Amenhotep seems to be concentrating on making his mark by enhancing or building more modest temples in the land, including those established in Nubia to reinforce Egypt's presence there. There are a few dramatic inscriptions on the walls of Karnak, and a few stone steles to be found here and there, in which the king boisterously brags about his accomplishments, but so far nothing great and mighty, including the two obelisks under construction. While one of the obelisks of Thutmose reaches a height of 205 cubits, Amenhotep's new matching pair will only be about 5 cubits – utterly minuscule in comparison! And instead of their being yet another remarkable contribution to the giant Karnak temple complex, they are to be set up just across the river on an island. They would only serve to grace the temple of the locally celebrated ram-headed creator god, Khnum.

The largest complete surviving Egyptian obelisk can be found in a plaza near a basilica in Rome. Known today as the 'Lateran Obelisk', it was commissioned by the pharaoh Thutmose III and installed at the Temple of Karnak in Thebes by his grandson, Thutmose IV. It was later removed to Italy by the Romans in the fourth century AD and erected in their sports arena, the Circus Maximus. The obelisk was 32.18 metres (70 cubits) with a weight of about 455 tons. Another obelisk which perhaps might have eventually been even larger remains in its quarry in Aswan today. With its shape roughed out and nearly freed from the surrounding rock, a large crack across its body seems to have doomed this project to abandonment.

Piay, who calls Thebes his home, remembers the arrival of one of the Thutmose obelisks when he was a child. There was much fanfare as the immense spire of stone arrived on a giant barge during the flood season, the water having risen high enough to bring it closer to the Karnak temple. The impressive barge was specifically built for its intimidating task, without tipping or sinking during loading, unloading and transport. Although he wasn't able to watch the actual installation process, Piay knew it involved a large number of men, and lots and lots of rope. Through ingenuity and strength, each obelisk would be dragged to its awaiting base, and then the shaft raised from a horizontal to vertical position.

⟵――――――――――――――――――――――――――――――⟶

In 1818, the flamboyant Italian explorer, Giovanni Belzoni (1778–1823), was commissioned to retrieve an obelisk found on the island of Philae south of Aswan. Hoping to transport it down the Nile and eventually to Britain, it was accidentally dropped into the Nile while it was in the process of being loaded on to a boat. Skilled in engineering, Belzoni was able to retrieve the obelisk and today it stands on the grounds of the Kingston Lacy estate in England. The inscriptions on this obelisk played a role in the process of deciphering the ancient Egyptian hieroglyphic script.

⟵――――――――――――――――――――――――――――――⟶

'Such a shame,' thinks Piay, who can only dream of being put in charge of such a project, and accordingly praised highly when successful. The magnificent obelisks of Thebes had all been derived from this very quarry. Instead, here are two puny contributions, weighing about 350 kilograms each. But of course he would never dare voice such thoughts out loud. When finished, Piay knows he will probably be able to touch their tops by standing on his toes and stretching his arm high. Nonetheless, he will do his job well, ensuring that the commission is fulfilled, and he will report to the vizier accordingly.

On the ground before him lies one of the blocks, three of its sides already smoothed and tapered, and its tip coming to a point. Among the background noise is the preparation of its twin not far away, its surfaces being pounded to match. Ignoring such distractions, Piay begins some of the work he came to accomplish, which includes providing the text for the carver who will ultimately embellish the little monuments. Before they could do that, though, the script needs to be traced on to the obelisks to guide their work. Piay hands his assistant, an artist named Ramose, a papyrus scroll on which the carefully worded text is written. After a few minutes of study, Ramose straddles the obelisk and, with pen and ink in hand, uses a straight edge to draw faint grid lines across the stone's surface. The lines will be used to set the size and symmetry for the text to follow.

Then, starting above near the top of the shaft, Ramose first sketches a depiction of Amenhotep kneeling and presenting offerings enclosed in two small pots to the god

Khnum. The hieroglyphs come next. Ramose unrolls the scroll to the proper portion and begins to transcribe the text between the lines he'd sketched. It isn't terribly complicated, with just a short inscription: 'Horus, The Mighty Bull, Great of Strength, the King of Upper and Lower Egypt, Aakheperure; Son of Re, Amenhotep, The Divine Ruler of Thebes. As a monument for his father, Khnum-Re, he made two obelisks for the altar of Re. May he celebrate the Gift of Life Ceremony forever.' Given the small size of the project, Ramose's work doesn't take long.

It would now be up to expert stonemasons to carefully incise the picture and words to produce a beautiful outcome, which would be done on site – after all, the obelisks were small and wouldn't be moved all that far. Piay and Ramose would be back in a few days to check on the progress and corrections would be made while they still could. When ready, the twins would bear a similar inscription and, much to Piay's dismay, the instructions requested that only one side on each be inscribed. 'Such a disappointment,' Piay mutters quietly so that no one else could hear. No towering monument, no giant barge, no dramatic installation in a sprawling temple. And probably no electrum embellishments; at such a small size, the precious metal would probably require protection from theft. Perhaps, he imagines and hopes, this is mere practice for a bigger project ahead, but given Amenhotep's record so far, he isn't counting on it.

Only eight royal obelisks remain in modern Egypt. Twenty-two are in other countries including France, Turkey and the United Kingdom. There are eight in Rome alone. Two that were commissioned by Thutmose III were nicknamed 'Cleopatra's Needles' in the nineteenth century and can be found in New York City's Central Park and on the banks of the Thames in London. Cleopatra lived over 1000 years after the obelisks were constructed but apparently the exotic reputation of Egypt and the ancient Greek queen of that land served to romanticize such impressive objects.

3RD HOUR OF THE DAY
(08.00–09.00)

THE FISHERMAN
BUILDS A SKIFF

… the Nile contains every variety of fish and in numbers beyond belief; for it supplies the natives not only with abundant subsistence, from the fish freshly caught, but it also yields an unfailing multitude for salting.

DIODORUS SICULUS, *The Library of History* **I:36**

Manu makes his way slowly towards the river, his eyes blurry from a night during which his sleep was constantly interrupted by the sounds of a baby coming into the world. Although cause for celebration, plenty of work still awaits those whose job it is to provide fish for the populace. Fortunately, the Nile rarely disappoints, and catfish, perch, tilapia and other popular edibles are typically abundant. Although one could throw a line and hook out from shore, the most effective techniques involves getting out into the water and the marshes along the river's banks, and that requires some sort of watercraft. The favourite of most is a simple skiff made from the stalks of papyrus plants. Manu's skiff is in sad shape. The day before, a couple of its chafed ropes had broken and a sizable chunk of the vessel had floated off downstream. It would have to be replaced and fortunately there is an endless supply of construction materials growing along the Nile.

Waiting near the water was Manu's friend, Ipuki, and his young son, Huy. The three often work together, spreading nets between their modest vessels and sharing the bounty. Today, they would be building a new skiff. The first step is to wade into the water and cut some fresh papyrus stalks to be deposited on the sandy bank. Ipuki volunteers to do the cutting, and Manu begins to grab armfuls and carry them to shore.

The ancient Egyptians did not refer to their river as the 'Nile', a word derived from the Greek *neilos*, meaning 'river valley'. They called it *itroo*, which simply means, 'the river', or *itroo-aa*, 'the great river'. The Egyptians believed it had its origins in waters running below a flat earth. Modern geographers explain that the river has two sources: one derived from melting snows in the highlands of Ethiopia, the so-called 'Blue Nile', and the other from lakes in Central Africa, the 'White Nile'. The two converge around Khartoum in modern-day Sudan. The natural cycle of the Nile in Egypt that once sustained the ancient civilization has now been radically disrupted with the building of an immense dam in the south. Today's Egyptians benefit from electricity, flood control and multiple growing seasons but they also require artificial fertilizers. And many archaeological sites threatened by the lake created by the dam required complete ancient temples to be rescued by moving them to higher ground.

Meanwhile, Huy is keeping dry on the bank, and Manu is glad to see that the boy is doing his job, scanning the surroundings. Although seemingly idyllic compared to some other professions, fishing has hazards worthy of respect. One could die any number of horrible deaths in the waters and marshlands of the Nile. Falling into the water and being swept away in a swift current is a constant fear, as is falling in and becoming tangled in a mesh of water plants. Of greatest concern, though, are two of the most terrifying animals in the land of Egypt: hippos and crocodiles.

Hippos are notoriously surly and their great size and large tusks can cause considerable damage to life and property. Every fisherman has his own story of close calls with the giant aquatic pig-like creatures who could bite through a skiff, and through those aboard as well. Over the years, several of Manu's friends have been killed directly or indirectly by hippos, which can stay submerged underwater for minutes only to ascend violently directly under their craft in what seemed to be intentionally malicious acts. With flailing bodies in the water, the hippo could have his way. Being plant-eaters, they have no particular interest in eating men, but will nonetheless cause havoc and traumatic injuries seemingly out of sheer meanness.

The hippos are a nuisance on land, too, Manu acknowledged. At night they emerge from the waters to continue feeding, and even with their short stubby legs, they can run fast and trample or bite anyone in their way. And they are a special nuisance to farmers, who sometimes find their crops violated by the hungry beasts. Occasionally a hunt is organized to rid an area of particularly annoying hippos but it is a very dangerous operation. True to form, the ruler, Amenhotep, has a public reputation for extraordinary and successful hunting, and is said to occasionally go out to the water to successfully subdue hippos with a harpoon. Manu isn't sure whether to believe the proclamations of the king's exploits. Is there anything sporty and dangerous that Amenhotep can't do better and bigger than anyone else? Anyway, keeping a look-out for large heads with twitching ears and big nostrils is essential.

The other menaces to be feared, crocodiles, are likewise of constant concern. They, too, have killed many, and are deadly, carnivorous, opportunistic feeders. Anything that comes into their path might be fair game including fish, birds and any inattentive land creature who might wander into the water or too close to shore. Crocodiles make little noise as they approached their prey and are known to have snatched small children playing near the river. Grasping their prey between their strong jaws, the crocs typically submerge their meals under the water and hold their quarry tight until they drown. Manu hopes that, as well as hippos, Huy is on the look-out for the tell-tale eyes gliding silently in their direction. Interestingly, both hippos and crocodiles would occasionally get into fights. With powerful jaws and natural weapons in their mouths, the battle is decided by size, speed and ferocity.

In an old Egyptian tale recorded on a surviving papyrus document, a priest who suspects his wife of cheating with a young man creates a magic crocodile out of wax. The croc turns to life and captures the suitor, holding him underwater for seven days, after which he was brought forth as evidence of the tryst. The wife and boyfriend were put to death and the crocodile reverted to its waxy self.

It isn't all frightening, though. The riverbanks and marshes are also home to a teeming variety of birds, which also could provide both food and sport. Hunting birds is a popular pastime of the elite, who would sometimes come out on fancy wooden skiffs, standing up, throwing stick or spear in hand, ready to knock out a few. It is a recreation for calm weather, with the deluxe skiff punted through the reeds and rushes while a seated servant or family member grasps the hunter's leg to steady him and hopefully prevent a most undesirable spill into the river.

Hippos are extinct in modern Egypt and crocodiles are found only in the far south in the lake formed by construction of the giant dam at Aswan. Still, they maintain their reputation as dangerous menaces today with hippos killing more people in Africa each year than any other animal, and crocodiles killing hundreds.

By now, Manu has laid a dozen armloads or so of papyrus stalks on the shore. The first step is to make rope. Taking several long stalks, the two fishermen lay them out and proceed to beat the papyrus flat with a mallet, the same one they use to beat unruly flopping fish taken aboard their vessel. Ipuki is an expert, and can produce strong cords in a process honed by years of experience. Huy feeds him fibres rendered from the crushed plants, which are then twisted between his father's palms. There are other plants in Egypt from which ropes could be made, but the papyrus stalks are best for the little skiffs. Such rope is easy to make, and being produced from a water-plant, it seems most suitable for surviving in an aquatic environment.

FISHERMEN MANUFACTURING SKIFFS FROM STALKS OF PAPYRUS

With sufficient coils of rope produced, the work has begun in earnest, but it will take at least the rest of the morning to complete. First, two fat bundles of the stalks will be laid out, with each end arranged to taper to a point. Winding the newly produced rope, each bundle will be tightly constricted and then secured with knots before they are compressed together to form a naturally buoyant sturdy platform with enough room for a couple of fishermen and their tools, along with baskets to hold their catch. The last step will be to pull up the ends and hold them in place with lines attached to the deck. The turned-up bow and stern will allow the skiff to ply the waters smoothly by pole or paddle.

In 1969, the Norwegian archaeologist and explorer, Thor Heyerdahl, built a large ship made of bundles of papyrus with an upturned bow and stern. With an international crew of seven, the boat was launched into the Atlantic Ocean to test the seaworthiness of such reed vessels which many ancient people seemed to have used. The boat, named *Ra*, rode the currents for weeks but disintegrated short of the Americas due to design flaws. The following year, a reconfigured *Ra II* was successful and another later experiment, an even larger vessel, was kept afloat for five months, thus demonstrating the possibility that such craft could have been effectively used for contact and trade in millennia past.

Manu has seen larger versions of his skiff now and again, almost all used for fishing, and the Nile hosts regular traffic of wooden boats of all sizes, especially at the port of Thebes. The diversity of cargo is impressive, from boats full of goods, both local and foreign, to huge chunks of stone quarried from far away. With their sails aloft they arrived upstream with the winds blowing from the north, sometimes with dozens of men rowing their oars, or travelling more easily with the current from the south. Curiously, many of the wooden boats have upturned prows and sterns that very much resemble papyrus vessels, perhaps a style touching back to the distant past, Manu speculates.

While working on the skiff, the three notice several

huge and impressive ships arriving on the east bank with great fanfare, shouting and noise. They are military vessels supporting what are likely to be some sort of expedition heading south, probably to Nubia. And then there is the occasional spectacle of the ruler's own magnificent ship with its falcon-headed prow and colourful streamers flying from its mast. Named *Aakheperure is the Establisher of the Two Lands*, it resembles a floating palace with the deck featuring a deluxe wooden cabin and all the luxuries one could imagine. The synchronized oars contribute to the majestic spectacle worthy of the Lord of the Two Lands as ordinary Egyptians line the river's banks in awe.

The skiff will be finished in a few more hours, a sturdy and effective vessel. The last bit of work will be to construct a couple of life-saving loops also made from papyrus. Laying out a narrow bundle of stalks, they will be tightly bound and their two ends tied together to form an oblong loop that could fit over one's arm and shoulder in the event of an unintentional plunge. Kept on the small deck, the device has saved many a life over the years. There was a close call a few months previously when a hippo rose up near Ipuki's skiff, causing a wave that knocked him into the water. He had been concentrating on tying some knots and never saw the beast coming. Young Huy grabbed for the life ring and in his panic, threw it in defence at the hippo rather than to his father. Ipuki quickly scrambled aboard with the message, 'Please don't tell your mother!'

After the skiff is finished, there will still be much to do – there are still fish to be caught. There is always the relatively lazy option of shore-fishing – throwing a line with a copper hook from the river bank – but the skiff is nearly always more effective and productive. Multiple hooks could be dropped off the little vessel and, with a little punting about, something would almost always turn up. Fish are abundant and desired, and a commodity easily traded in the village for life's other necessities. Taken ashore, they could be grilled or split open for drying on racks. And unlike beef, fish is cheap and available to almost anyone.

Manu often carries a spear with him for the occasional opportunity to skewer a large fish in shallower water. He could drag it behind his skiff to shore while hoping that a croc wouldn't take a chunk out of it. Net fishing, though, is always the most productive. Nets thrown skilfully into the water and retrieved in short order usually turn up something, but some of the biggest yields he has ever gathered were a result of working in cooperation with Ipuki. With identical skiffs, the two would spread a broad net between the two vessels and anything and everything drifting by would get caught – mostly fish. The nets require constant inspection and repair but the effort is definitely worthwhile. They both take great delight in coming ashore with baskets loaded with fish from which they would select the best for their families before trading away the rest with others.

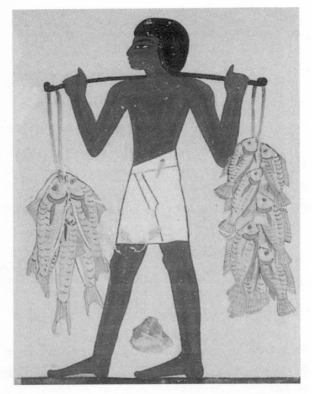

DELIVERING SOME DELICIOUS NILE FISH

'Ready to get out the nets?' Manu jokes to his friend – there is a long way to go before the boat is river-worthy.

4TH HOUR OF THE DAY
(09.00–10.00)

THE POTTER
SHAPES SOME CLAY

The potter is covered with dirt while still living.
He rummages in the ground more than a pig to bake
his pots. His clothes are stiff with mud, his head–cloth is
made of rags, and he inhales the scorching air from his
blazing furnace.

Satire of the Trades

Itu, with his wife Nani, lives in a small dilapidated two-room mud-brick home with a hanging sheet of linen serving as a front door. Childless, Itu is sure they seem dedicated to each other, but less so to their work. Both hate their occupations, but such is life. Itu spends the day in a pottery workshop being splattered with mud and breathing hot, acrid fumes while Nani makes a living manufacturing linen loincloths. Every so often the two argue over whose lot is the worst. Sadly for Itu, potters are considered very low down on the social scale, somewhere akin to, but maybe slightly higher than, brick-makers. It is the muck and filth of the job that has given it such a bad reputation. 'But I make underwear for a living,' Nani would counter. 'All day long nearly every day.' And they both agree that they are vastly underpaid given their efforts and the importance of their output.

Itu's father had been a potter and so had most of the male members of his family going back as far as anyone could remember. A city the size of Thebes with its numerous workers, temples and tombs perpetually requires pots for dozens of different uses. The average Egyptian needs vessels for storing food and water, cups for drinking, and plates for serving meals. The elite need their wine jars, and the temples need their storage and ritual vessels. The dead, too, require ceramic items to accompany them in the Afterlife or for offerings left at their tombs. And there is the constant need for beer jugs used in payment for working. There is, too, the fact that no matter how well made, pots could and would eventually break. As a result, there are a large number of pottery workshops in the region.

It all starts with the retrieval and treatment of the clay from the river banks. Intrusive material such as small rocks and other bits of unwanted debris could be sorted but other materials such as sand or chaff might be added to the mix to temper the clay for shaping. Shaping is usually done on a wheel that could be turned by hand to produce uniformity. After the newly created and wet pot is finished, it is set out to dry and when its surface is still malleable, it could be burnished smooth or otherwise polished and additional features could be added such as decorative motifs or colour.

Complete and fragmentary pots are a major source of archaeological information. Like automobiles and clothing trends, the styles of pots changed through time and an expert in ceramics can tell, sometimes quite precisely, when a pot was made. Pot shards tend to survive well through time because pots are ubiquitous as they are readily broken and then replaced. The study of pottery is especially useful in areas where there is a lack of suitable inscriptions for dating a site. In Egypt, for example, it assists greatly in determining the age of domestic sites, or burials without decoration. Egyptian pots found in other lands can provide clues to possible trade or other interactions, as can imported pottery found in Egypt, sometimes as containers for costly products from abroad.

When completely dry, it is time to bake the pots hard. The workshop where Itu is employed has a large kiln made from bricks that allows dozens of vessels to be fired at the same time. Each is set into the kiln and placed or stacked on a platform designed to hold the items. With everything ready, a fire is lit from a small chamber below, fuelled by straw, dried animal dung or other flammable materials.

There is a good reason that the pottery workshops and kilns are located a distance away from the village. The kilns can produce irritating smoke and a bad smell that few appreciate. Having spent most of his life in such an environment, Itu barely notices it. It can be dangerous at times, too, with serious burns ever possible when working around an oven heated to high temperatures. Even so, he is rarely involved in the firing itself or the collection of fuel. Having started out as a lad fetching clay or kneading it with water with his feet in a vat, he could now usually be found on the turning wheel as his abilities are regarded as competent, if not acknowledged. Still, like his fellow potters, his pay was paltry, unlike the owner of the workshop who was clearly wealthy, appearing at times from a distance in his immaculate clothing.

Now, during the fourth hour of the day, Itu has already been at work for a couple of hours, and has produced dozens of shallow plates. As usual, the supervisor arrived demanding Itu create hundreds of large storage jars, a task that will take him and his fellow potters a good many days.

Unlike simple plates, cups and small containers that could be produced in a matter of minutes, the big vessels require much more time to build and shape the wet clay to produce the desired outcome.

Some ancient water jars were made to be semi-porous. The evaporation of moisture on the outside of the pots would keep the liquid inside cool. Such vessels, often known as *zirs*, are still used in the Middle East today.

After years of repetition, making clay items is almost automatic, and often Itu will drift off into daydreams and then awaken to find a finished pot between his muddy hands. The themes of his reveries are often the same: fantasies about having some other profession. Even fishing looks more interesting, with each day having a degree of unpredictability. Occasionally, though, he thinks about his general lot in life and as he started one of the new pots, he considers the plight of his wife.

Nani had had a better life at one time, living at home with her doting parents, but it soon came to an end when she fell in love with Itu. Her parents were appalled and when she moved in with him, thus creating a marriage and a household, they essentially disowned her. Itu's parents, though, utterly approved as in their eyes, their son was improving his station in life, but such was not to be the case.

Nani's profession was equally repetitive. Making loincloths was pretty much the same day after day. At that very moment, Itu knew she would be cutting linen of various qualities into triangular shapes and then hemming their edges with thread and needle. With their three corners tied together, the garment is the simplest ever and is worn by many workers as their primary outfit.

POTTERS AT WORK

He knows Nani, too, often looks with envy at the work of others, even in her own workshop. Those working the looms seem to her far more engaged if not slightly happier and she said it reminds her of her own mother, who had had a small loom in their family home. Unlike the large vertical apparatus in the workshop, the home loom was horizontal and set up on the floor. She told how her mother would spin the flax fibres into thread, which was then arranged in the loom to be woven over and under repeatedly to produce suitable sheets. Her father, who was a supervisor of tomb construction, usually wore a kilt every day, which was merely a length of the homemade fabric wrapped around his waist a few times and then tucked or tied, with or without a loincloth beneath. Sometimes he would wear a long tunic, essentially a loose dress coming down to below his knees and with sleeves and a hemmed hole for his head and neck. It was simple but looked far more sophisticated than anything worn by the average worker – certainly Itu has nothing of the like.

Yes, he knows that in some ways Nani's life had once been far better before she fell for his charms, and the lovely dresses she once wore at her parent's home are no more. There are, though, occasional perks to her job. While cutting and hemming underwear all day is rewarded with a few jugs of beer and some bread, she is allowed, from time to time, to take away a few bits of coarser cloth that have developed holes, and thus can sew some clothing at home, or hang a sheet as a door.

←——————————————————————————→

Linen was derived from the flax plant, which was grown in vast fields all over Egypt. The cloth produced from it could vary in quality depending on when the flax was harvested. The green plants produced fine, softer threads while that from the more yellow and mature stalks were tougher and thicker. Pulling up the flax was followed by a tedious process of combing and soaking the stems to release and soften the fibres, and ultimately spinning would produce thread that could be used in manufacturing several qualities of linen. The finest, softest and most expensive was gauze-like and suitable for the elite, while the others varied from softer to coarser, the latter being the most affordable.

Itu snaps out of his daydreams when a thick splash of mud from the spinning wheel slaps him across the face. The process of working with wet hands and clay always makes a mess. It is impossible not to be coated with muck from head to toe, at least on one's front. As it quickly dries on both skin and clothes under the hot Egyptian sun, it could develop a kind of crust that would require more than a little effort to scrub out. There are times when Itu arrives home looking like a kind of brown ceramic figure, sometimes naked, but too tired or too lazy to scrub himself off in the river. Feeling lethargic so early in the day increases the chance that such a scenario will likely be the case once again tonight and, as usual, he will vow to clean up on the following day. Hopefully Nani will have some food ready for him so he can exhaustedly drift off, no doubt haunted by unrealistic dreams of another profession – even making loincloths might be preferable.

5TH HOUR OF THE DAY
(10.00–11.00)

THE SCRIBAL
STUDENT ANTICIPATES
HIS BEATING

I will make you love books more than your own mother ...
The scribal profession is greater than any other. There is
nothing like it on earth.

Satire of the Trades

Nakht winces. He can't remember one of the signs needed
to write a particular word. It is one of three choices, all
birds, and each representing radically different sounds in
the language. It would be just a matter of time before a

mistake would be detected and he would feel the harsh crack of a switch across his back. Sitting on the floor of the open-roofed walled enclosure, 'the House of Instruction', he wracks his mind, hoping to remember what he was expected to know by now. Scribal school certainly isn't easy, with hundreds of signs to be precisely drawn with no mistakes tolerated. Being a scribe is quite a responsibility. With few in Egypt able to read or write, it is also a powerful profession involving a lot of trust; those who are illiterate are utterly dependent upon the scribes to write or read documents in an accurate and truthful matter.

It's difficult to estimate the rate of literacy in ancient Egypt. Some estimates suggest it was as low as 3 per cent. While the average Egyptian could get through life quite well without knowing how to read or write, it was an essential skill for the masses of bureaucrats and many priests who served the complex civil and religious administration during the New Kingdom. While the scribal schools were filled with boys, there is evidence that some women were literate, most probably those from elite families.

Nakht looks around the room at his fellow students. Most of them, all boys, are the sons of prominent members of society, many of whom are overseers or accountants, and all are expected to follow in their fathers' bureaucratic footsteps. Nakht's father is a prominent physician, and the ability to consult medical texts mandates that reading, at least, is essential. Others anticipate a career as tomb artists or supervisors of the sculptors who would carve bold hieroglyphs into large, permanent monuments of stone.

The plethora of hieroglyphs is intimidating. The script being learned could be written from left to right, right to left or even top to bottom, and it is a less formal, somewhat abbreviated type of writing than the often detailed hieroglyphs found inscribed on royal or religious monuments and objects.

'Why so many signs to tell apart?' Nakht foolishly asks his instructor, Nebamun. 'It works, doesn't it?' comes the stern reply. 'You can read it, can you not? Don't you enjoy learning? Maybe you should catch fish or make bricks!' Nakht instantly feels the sting of Nebamun's switch and yet again makes a mental note to ask questions of content rather than curiosity. And, as a kind of pedagogical punishment, Nebamun announces to all that because of the impertinent question, there is yet again a need to reinforce the notion of how privileged they are to receive a scribe's education. Once again, the students are to take dictation on the subject of the virtues of being a scribe. Nebamun will recite and the students are expected to perfectly transcribe what they hear, while repeating it in unison in a rhythmical, singsong chant.

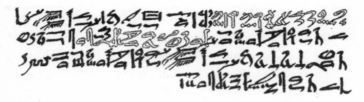

THE CURSIVE EGYPTIAN SCRIPT

'You will write the following,' commands Nebamun. 'I have seen a coppersmith at work at the mouth of a furnace. His fingers were like the claws of a crocodile and he stank more than fish eggs. Write it and repeat it now!'

Nakht picks up a large broken shard of a pot, and wets the end of his pen in a small jug of water before dipping it into the ink on his palette. The palette, a narrow block of wood with a couple of depressions on its surface, was a gift from his father, and allows him to write in either black or red. Nebamun would rarely allow the newer students to use paper. It is far costlier than pieces of shattered jars, which can be found in great quantities in any village, or random flakes of limestone with their white surfaces. Piles of both lie in a heap in the corner of the compound. Occasionally, the students are allowed to use wooden writing boards, which would be of use when they eventually join the ranks of the professionals. The boards are covered with a surface of washed plaster allowing for writing to be erased with water, or plastered over with another coat.

The Egyptian god of writing, wisdom and knowledge was Thoth, who could be depicted as a baboon and, more commonly, as an ibis-headed man. He is often seen holding a scribe's palette and pen, or taking notes in scenes in the Book of the Dead during which the deceased is experiencing judgement. A goddess, Seshat, also represented writing, along with accounting and mathematics.

The dull pen tip has left an ugly blotch on the ceramic surface and Nakht quickly grabs another less blunt pen tucked behind his ear. Essentially a stick made from a thin slice of reed, such pens are simple, but they certainly require skill in their use. With his eyes turned down in concentration, he begins to write the flowing characters. The words are mostly familiar; he has taken this particular condescending dictation several times and is more or less comfortable with the spellings.

'Carpenters work harder than most. The barber shaves until late in the day. Wandering down street after street, he seeks more customers. He wears out his arms to fill his belly.'

The students write as elegantly and quickly as they are able, and try to recite clearly in unison, with no one lagging behind nor copying his neighbour – at least obviously. Nakht knows what is coming next: a nasty and snobbish assessment of arrow makers, potters and bricklayers.

'The arrowmaker travels north to the Delta and works hard. When gnats sting him and the sand fleas bite him, he'll hate his life. The potter is covered with earth and looks like a dead man. He roots in the earth more than a pig. His clothes are stiff with mud, and his nose is burned by the searing heat of the furnace. Bricklayers ... their kidneys hurt. Even when it's cold and windy, they work outside mostly naked. His strength has disappeared due to fatigue and stiffness. He eats bread with his fingers, although he only washes once a day.'

The list continues, with several necessary professions including weavers, farmers and fishermen, all of whom, according to Nebamun, live utterly miserable existences. 'Now repeat after me and then write it down: If you understand writing, then it will be better for you than all other professions. A day at school is worthwhile.'

Nakht flips over the pot shard and continues the exercise by writing on the back as Nebamun wanders about the enclosure, looking over the shoulders of his nervous but earnest students. The occasional snap of the switch indicates that mistakes are being made. Nakht averages about three strikes a week. The switch certainly hurts and is a genuine incentive to pay attention, concentrate and be serious. Occasionally the students would debate among themselves as to which hurt more: the slender switch made from a date palm branch or Nebamun's wooden staff. Breaking into tears would result in an additional swat, and although one's mother might offer some sympathy, most fathers do not: they experienced the same themselves. Nakht's father, Neferhotep, had even been taught by Nebamun himself over thirty years previously.

Although a harsh master, Nebamun is very well respected in Thebes. When not teaching, he could often be seen seated in a shady place, busy at work. His crossed legs pulled his linen skirt taut, providing him with a flat, sturdy writing surface. He had held a variety of trusted positions over the years, and even taught writing to the young Amenemopet, now the vizier of the ruler. His expertise is widely sought, and apart from teaching writing, he is often commissioned to write copies of the Book of the Dead, a papyrus scroll bearing instructions for the deceased on how to endure the journey into the Netherworld and successfully survive judgment before the gods. Such a scroll is expensive but highly desired by those of the elite who could afford such insurance. And Nebamun is trusted for his integrity. While other scribes are known to sloppily compose funerary texts, knowing full well that their creation would be rolled up, placed in a jar and sealed in a tomb, never to be seen, Nebamun takes great care.

Nebamun uses only the best materials for this work, including high-quality paper manufactured from the papyrus plant. Those gathering the plant cut stalks near their base before removing their tops, binding them together to be carried in bundles on their back. At the workshop, the green outer skin of the plant is removed, and the fibrous inner pith cut into thin strips. The strips are laid out on a flat surface with their edges overlapping and a second set of strips, likewise with overlapping edges, is placed atop and parallel to the first. The strips could be pressed between planks with heavy rocks or bricks, and the natural adhesives in the plant material would bind the fibres into a strong paper. A single sheet could be glued to the edges of others to make a scroll as long as necessary.

The Roman naturalist, Pliny the Elder (AD 23–79), wrote the following in his description of Egypt: 'We must make some mention of the nature of the papyrus, seeing that all the usages of civilized life depend in such a remarkable degree upon the employment of paper – at all events, the remembrance of past events' (*Natural History*, Vol. 3, Chapter 21). In fact, during the period when Egypt was subjugated by the Greek and Roman empires, it became a major exporter of paper to the civilized ancient world. As climate changed over the many centuries since, the papyrus plant became essentially extinct in Egypt, the land which made it famous, and was only brought back in modern times with the establishment of a few commercial plantations for the purpose of providing novelty paper as tourist souvenirs.

Nakht began school at age eight and now, at ten years old, feels he is becoming rather good. In two more years, he will be finished with the basic course. Several days ago, he learned to write a variety of words by categories: places, people, plants, etc., after which the students had learned some arithmetic. The latter is his least favourite subject but many scribes are expected to record things such as war booty, temple property, donations and crop yields, and even to master the computations needed for engineering operations such as the transport of stone and building of monuments. It is a very useful skill for maintaining an empire.

Still looking intently down, Nakht can hear the footsteps of his teacher moving behind a line of seated boys, looking over their shoulders for any mistake. The shuffling feet stop behind him. 'Wrong bird!' shouts Nebamun. Nakht knows what is coming next. Whack! The word would never be forgotten again.

THE PRIESTESS OF HATHOR GETS DRUNK

[The pharaoh] comes to dance and he comes to sing ... his sistrum is made of gold and his necklace is made of malachite. His feet dance for the Mistress of Music. He dances for her and she loves it!

'Hymn to Hathor', TEMPLE OF DENDERAH

Hathor is a complicated goddess and everyone knows it. Often depicted as a cow, or as a woman with a sun disc between horns, or a woman with cow ears, she appears in many forms and goes by many names. At times, she is a loving nurturer and a mother-figure to the ruler, yet she has a very violent streak as well. Sometimes Hathor is called the 'Golden One', or she could be associated with fertility, or with trees and marshes, or with places such as the turquoise mines of the Sinai or even the land of the dead in the west where the sun sets. And she could be variously described as the wife, mother or even daughter of the sun god Re, and was thus associated with many events celebrating him. She is the goddess of music and she loves to get drunk. Yes, Hathor has many roles in many places.

On the sixth hour of this particular day, Ty is already drunk at home, much to the distress of her husband. 'Why do you do this?' she is asked, for what feels to her like the hundredth time.

'I'm a priestess of Hathor, silly man. I'm doing my duty. I'm practising!' And that is the only explanation she is going to give.

Indeed, as a priestess of Hathor, based in Thebes, Ty keeps busy participating in many of the festivals with which the goddess is associated, and those in which she is directly honoured. There are many dramatic and often joyous festivals held in Egypt each year, to which everyone could look forward. Each temple in the land has its own celebrations in honour of its gods, but Thebes, home to the dominant deity, Amun-Re, holds the largest and most elaborate. For example, there is the famous annual Opet (or

'Secret Chamber') Festival, during which the god Amun-Re actually leaves the confines of his secluded, secretive chamber at the rear of the Karnak temple. His image is placed in a shrine affixed to a small wooden ship, which is carried on poles by a sturdy group of priests. Making its way through the various parts of the temple and into the sunlight, the 'sacred barque' eventually makes its way out of the temple compound where it is greeted by enthusiastic crowds of people lining the streets keen to have a look. It's the closest thing an average Egyptian will have to actually experiencing the gods, given that their inhabited images are kept secure in their temples most of the time.

The ship is preceded and followed by lively groups of musicians and dancers who all but guarantee a festive occasion. Drums are pounded along with tambourines and the sounds of flutes and even harps can be heard in the mix. Acrobats do turns in the street while a dozen priestesses sing and clap. Ty is one of those priestesses and she loves every minute of these processions. With a sistrum, a symbol of Hathor, shaking in her hand, she represents the goddess with music and dance.

←——————————————————————————→

The sistrum is a type of rattle typically featuring a handle holding a lyre-like structure bearing metal discs that would clack together. The handles could feature the bovine face of Hathor, thus emphasizing her association with music. Rattling could also be produced by shaking marsh plants. Ivory clappers, often in the shape of arms with hands, were also popular and could make quite a racket when slapped together.

Each year, the Opet Festival procession stops here and there along its route, sometimes visiting other temples, or just pausing. It gives a great opportunity for additional adoration and ecstatic appreciation, and it also gives the carrying crew a rest before moving on. At the end of his journey, Amun-Re would be placed back into his shrine in the temple to receive the daily attentions of his assigned priests, and the public would have special memories to share while eagerly awaiting the next festival.

Another huge temple ('Luxor Temple') would be built in Thebes a few kilometres away from Karnak. Much of it was built by the pharaoh Amenhotep III, a grandson of Amenhotep II. During his long reign, Egypt's vast wealth would be ostentatiously displayed with impressive construction projects throughout the land. With the new temple established, a causeway lined with stone sphinxes would connect the temples and thereafter, the Barque of Amun would travel between the two during the Opet Festival.

Living in Thebes, Ty is married to a royal steward who works for the palace. His influence helped her to be selected as a priestess, an office she serves as needed, and one she rather enjoys, especially because she, like Hathor, loves to be drunk. There are certain festivals during which becoming inebriated is almost a requirement, and Ty is more than pleased to be involved both in the planning of the events and the participation of the Hathor priestesses. Two are her special favourites: the Valley Feast and the Festival of Drunkenness.

The Valley Feast involves the images of the god Amun-Re, along with his wife and son, Mut and Khonsu, being placed on ceremonial barques at Karnak, and crossing the river to visit the various memorial temples on the west bank of the Nile. These memorial temples belong to the deceased rulers preceding the present pharaoh, Amenhotep, including a monument for his own father, the third Thutmose. Each has their own priesthood whose duty it is to honour the king who is still a god in death as he had been in life. The most beautiful of the memorial temples hugged the base of a massive cliff. Awkwardly, it belongs to the censored female ruler, Hatshepsut. Its walls record her many achievements but her name has been expunged, her images smashed, and her priesthood dissolved. It is still worth a visit, as Ty has done many times. A shrine to Hathor was built on to the temple, even though it was clear that Hatshepsut had used a symbolic association with the goddess to legitimize her unconventional reign.

Gods carried in procession could also serve as oracles. It has been recorded that during public processions of Amun-Re in his shrine on the sacred barque, observers could ask yes/no questions to the deity. If the barque borne on the priests' shoulders dipped slightly forward, the answer was affirmative, if backward, then negative. Those who are cynical might suggest that this was an opportunity for manipulation by the priests, or was it just a matter of the bearers adjusting the heavy weight on their shoulders?

Ty and her sistrum-rattling priestesses provide festive sound and motion at each stop of the Valley Feast where praises are sung to Amun-Re and his family, and the deceased, as they spiritually celebrate each other. There would always be plenty to eat and drink at each stop. Ty especially enjoys the fine wine provided at the temple dedicated to the memory of the first Thutmose, and always makes sure she has her fill. The singers and dancers continue throughout the tour, but soon their songs tend to become louder and somewhat slurred, and their dancing less precise. It isn't only priests and their entourage who are involved in the Valley Feast. It is an opportunity for any Egyptian to pay respects at the graves of their deceased relatives.

Although many rulers of the New Kingdom built memorial temples to celebrate themselves in perpetuity, few survive today. Some involved the extensive use of mud-brick, which deteriorates if not maintained, or featured stone blocks that were quarried away in later years for use in other projects. Very little remains of the memorial temples of such New Kingdom luminaries as Thutmose III and Amenhotep II. Much of the grandiose memorial temple of Amenhotep III was destroyed in an earthquake and its stones used elsewhere. Two immense seated statues were most of what remained until recent excavations, which have revealed much more of the temple. The temples of later rulers including Seti I, Rameses II and Rameses III were built mostly of stone and have survived well to this day but, ironically, one of the best-preserved from the earlier part of the New Kingdom is that of Hatshepsut, whose memory was supposed to have been erased.

Those carrying the sacred barques are expected to remain pure and sober, and although they might indulge in some of the delicious food provided, they are not to become intoxicated; the trio of gods require smooth and reliable transport, and cannot be dropped. In most Valley Feasts, some of Ty's fellow priestesses fall out along the way, too drunk to continue, and the entourage returning to Karnak is usually noticeably smaller.

The last Valley Feast was certainly memorable in that Ty could recall the details, and she couldn't wait for the Festival of Drunkenness, as she repeatedly tells her husband in her late-morning stupour. He doesn't look pleased. But Ty has an important position and, now in her mid-thirties, has been performing her role admirably for a number of years. Besides, in the Festival of Drunkenness, all over the land Egyptians get drunk and celebrate the gifts of Hathor, her husband included. Dancing and singing are expected, and drinking alcohol is mandatory. It really is better than the Valley Feast, Ty has concluded, as there isn't a lot of travel involved. In Thebes, one can celebrate in the streets, as most do, but for a truly ecstatic experience, a visit to the temple dedicated to the goddess Mut, the wife of Amun-Re, is necessary. If Amun-Re was considered the king of the gods, then Mut is certainly the queen.

THE GODDESS HATHOR

Hathor's association with Mut can be linked to her fiercely protective and motherly qualities and her religious association with Re. An ancient Egyptian tale relates how Re became tired of humans so he set off to destroy them. As an enthusiastic participant, his daughter, Hathor, transformed herself first into the vengeful Eye of Re, and then into the vicious goddess Sekhmet, who is often depicted as a violent and intimidating lioness. As such, she enthusiastically participated in the slaughter and enjoyed the blood and carnage. Soon, Re felt sorry for his actions and, to stop the murder, he had to control Hathor. He did so by having a huge quantity of beer dyed red and having it poured into the fields. The goddess, thirsty and thinking it was human blood, sucked it up, became inebriated and passed out. Thus humanity was saved from complete destruction ... by beer. The Festival of Drunkenness celebrates this redemption and while Egyptian morals generally advocate sobriety in daily life, parties and special celebrations are the exception. This particular festival also encourages drunken and public intimate encounters with friends or strangers, something normally frowned upon.

In another Egyptian story, the sun god Re is depressed and many attempts to cheer him up have failed. The happy conclusion to the story results from Hathor presenting herself before Re, and opening her robe to reveal her naked body. Re found this so amusing that he broke into hysterical laughter. Why this was funny can only be conjectured, but it did the trick, and Re got over his poor spirits.

THE PREDICTABLE RESULTS OF TOO MUCH CELEBRATING WITH HATHOR

Every year, Ty and her husband make their way to the Mut temple where copious amounts of drink await. With years of experience behind her, she always paces herself so as to stay genuinely drunk, but not to the point of total dysfunction, unlike some of her fellow celebrants. She also hates vomiting and never wishes to reach that point, but she does want to reach the point of falling asleep in the temple precinct. Apart from enjoying the inebriation, it is the hope of many that they will experience an encounter with Hathor herself in a sacred space – a rare ecstatic personal encounter with the divine. Ty never would admit that she has yet to achieve such a special experience, and isn't sure if her friends were telling her the truth when they shared theirs. Regardless, there is always that annual hope.

Each year, the worst part is the next morning when she and all those who had passed-out on the temple grounds are awakened by the loud pounding of a drum. Many would have hangovers and prefer to be left alone, but the festival would be over and it would be time to move on. Ty would look around for her husband and hope not to find him unconscious and in the arms of another woman, but this particular celebration seems to excuse such excesses.

◄──►

The site of Denderah in Egypt was used as a sacred space for several millennia including as a special place for the worship of Hathor. Today, it features one of the best preserved temples from ancient times anywhere, and it was dedicated to the goddess. Much of it was built by the Greeks and Romans who themselves had incorporated Egyptian gods into their religion.

◄──►

On this specific day during the harvest season, the major drinking festivals are over although there will be many other opportunities for excessive behaviour. Ty and her husband are popular party guests, and Hathor, by nature, would expect her priestesses to have a good time. Happily, there is one such celebration tonight, at the home of an overseer named Userhet and, with any luck, the wine will be fine and Ty can once again practise in the name of Hathor.

7TH HOUR OF THE DAY

(12.00–13.00)

THE VIZIER HEARS REPORTS

Regarding the exact procedure of His Excellency the Vizier when he gives a hearing in the Hall of the Vizier. He is to sit on a backed chair, a reed mat being on the ground, the chain of office on him, a skin under his back, another under his feet, and a mat-work cape on him, a baton near him, forty leather rods laid out before him, the Chiefs of Ten of Upper Egypt before him on either hand, the chamberlain on his right hand, the Controller of Ingress on his left, and the scribes of the Vizier near him.

'The Duties of the Vizier', TOMB OF REKHMIRE

He has only been at work in his palace office for a few hours but already Amenemopet is growing weary from the barrage of details and decisions he's had to face this day. As the vizier to Amenhotep, he is the ruler's right-hand man and his responsibilities are both vast and paramount. Second only to the king, he is well rewarded for his efforts and enjoys many of the luxuries, benefits and wealth one would expect of his station, but the work is endless. Not one to complain too much, he long ago concluded that he works longer and harder than Amenhotep who of course was the ultimate decision maker – after all, Amenhotep is the divine king and saddled with the task of maintaining divine order in the universe, at least to the benefit of Egypt.

It helps to be a best friend of the ruler, the two having grown up together. That relationship was, in fact, the basis for his appointment. The previous ruler's vizier, Rekhmire, had served quite ably and Amenhotep had kept him in that post for a while at the beginning of his reign. But Rekhmire was getting older and was also a part of what appeared to be a growing dynasty of hereditary viziers. Amenhotep put an end to that by appointing Amenemopet. Another of the king's close friends, Sennefer, is Amenemopet's brother, and likewise holds a high position: mayor of the vitally important city of Thebes. It seems that the ruler values friendship and loyalty over hereditary traditions when it comes to choosing his closest advisors and administrators.

It was the usual case in Egyptian administration to have two viziers serving under the ruler: one with a jurisdiction over Lower Egypt (the Delta region) and a second with authority over Upper Egypt (the Nile valley). In the case of Amenhotep II, Egyptologists have found evidence for only one, Amenemopet, and it's possible that he bore responsibilities for the entire land.

Amenemopet's job is complicated. He receives reports from dozens of overseers of this and that and provides regular reports to the ruler. Although he is free to make numerous decisions on his own, those of personal interest to Amenhotep, or of vital concern to Egypt, would be made by the ruler himself. The vizier is also expected to hear and decide the most important of judicial cases, mostly those of rulings from lower magistrates that were now being appealed. And apart from that, he is expected to manage the royal estates, including the palace and its security, and monitor the treasury. Fortunately, the vast hierarchical bureaucracy beneath him takes care of most of the details.

The morning has certainly been busy and it would only be getting busier. Already he has heard reports from the treasurer, the Overseer of Granaries and the Overseer of Fields. The treasurer, Djehutynefer, presented his findings while several of Amenemopet's scribes sat on the floor taking notes. Djehutynefer came with his own entourage of scribes, some holding scrolls full of tallies while others recorded the proceedings. The news had been good, as it usually is, with the state coffers bursting with the fruits of empire. With special thanks to Amenhotep and his father, Thutmose, tribute from foreign lands under Egypt's domination is regularly flowing in and that trend is to be maintained to support the various building schemes and the opulence of the ruler himself.

SCRIBES TAKING NOTES

The Overseer of Granaries had had similarly positive news. The state-owned granaries are sufficiently full to feed those under its employ until the next harvest, plus a surplus. Bread and beer would be available without worry. There are some concerns with the physical maintenance of several of the immense storage silos on the outskirts of Thebes. A couple have domed tops ready to collapse thus threatening to expose the stored grain to the elements and consumption by birds and rats. 'You are authorized to repair or replace them immediately,' Amenemopet had instructed.

It was quite common for elite bureaucrats to have had many titles, which were often cumulatively listed on the walls of their tomb regardless of whatever position they might have had at the time of their death. The titles of Amenemopet, vizier of Amenhotep II include: Chief of the Entire Land, Overseer of Foremost Lands, Priest of Maat, One Who Hears in the Six Great Houses, Controller of All Kilts and Master of the Secrets of the West. His predecessor, Rekhmire, recorded over thirty, including Overseer of the Double Gold Treasuries and of the Double Silver Treasuries, Overseer of Crafts, Overseer of Archives, Master of Secrets of the Palace and 'He of the Curtain'.

Next, the Overseer of Fields made his appearance. One of his scribes had carried a heavy bundle of a half-dozen scrolls or so, cradled on his outstretched arms. Although Amenemopet appreciated the overseer's reports, he found them routinely tedious. Much of the information usually centred on taxation of various kinds of land parcels both privately maintained or owned by the state. Of course, there are untold thousands of fields of all sizes in all parts of Egypt, and a portion of their produce, especially grain, would be given up for the state and temple silos. Quantities of cattle, too, often feature in his reports and sometimes the vizier feels the overseer just likes to talk. It is clear that he enjoys his regular visits to the palace and perhaps wishes to prolong them. At some point, Amenemopet would always grow impatient and would ask for the grand summary, which in his opinion would still take too long to report.

This time, the long-winded Overseer had had an additional issue to present in the form of a land dispute between two prominent owners of large productive fields. Apparently a boundary marker had been moved to someone's disadvantage. Ironically, the boundary movement slightly diminished the size of the plot of the alleged perpetrator, placing a path used by a hippo well within the fields of his neighbour. The regular trampling had had an effect on productivity, and the neighbour was still expected to pay taxes based on the size of his plots. The case had been brought to a local judge who ruled in favour of the defendant but now the plaintiff was appealing to the vizier himself.

Amenemopet was already familiar with both parties. It seemed that every other year some dispute or other of theirs made its way up through the system to land in his lap. The vizier took a moment or two to consider the case before rendering a verdict. As there was no extraordinary compelling evidence, his verdict was simple, if not punitive to both. The new boundary marker would be established in the centre of the hippo track. Amenemopet's personal scribe wrote out the decision and handed it to the overseer before dismissing him with an irritated remark: 'And I don't ever want to hear from either of those two again nor anything involving hippos!'

> *Do not displace the surveyor's marker on the boundaries of the arable land, nor alter the position of the measuring line. Do not covet a single cubit of land, nor encroach on the boundaries of a widow, for one who transgresses the furrow shortens a lifetime, and one who acquires by deceptive means, will be lassoed by the might of the moon ... Be careful not to topple over the boundary markers of the fields, not fearing that you will be brought to court.*
>
> **The Instruction of Amenemopet**

Already exhausted from tedium, the one official that the vizier actually finds fascinating is the Overseer of Royal Works, who now comes before him. Receiving updates on the construction of such things as temples, palaces and royal statuary would always feel like progress was being made and even the occasional problems could involve challenging but satisfying solutions. There are two small obelisks being created at a quarry down south, and a new palace being built up north, both of which were reported to be successfully underway. Of special interest is the construction of Amenhotep's own royal tomb in the Place of Secrets, the royal cemetery whose details are known but to a few. As vizier, Amenemopet has been privileged to visit the building site on a number of occasions as the tomb has gradually grown in size. And on a personal note, he had previously asked the overseer to put an architect and work crew to work on building his own tomb in the growing cemetery for wealthy bureaucrats. His predecessor, Rekhmire, had certainly done so and the tomb of his brother, Sennefer, was well underway.

The tomb of Amenemopet's predecessor, Rekhmire, is incredibly decorated with scenes of crafts and professional activities of all sorts, some of which serve as illustrations in this book. The tomb of his brother, Sennefer, is likewise extraordinary, with smoothed and plastered irregularities in its ceiling allowing for the painting of grape clusters with a feeling of three dimensions.

Amenemopet's tomb would be carved into the rock next to the tomb of his brother and it would be on a par with his status as a vizier. Its chapel walls would be covered with texts noting his accomplishments and scenes of a splendid Afterlife. It is far from being finished but hopefully all would be in order on that unknown day when his own mummification was complete and his body was ready to be installed therein for eternity.

The meeting with the Overseer of Royal Works is a short, pleasant and refreshing exchange, and when the official departs, Amenemopet traverses the palace to the king's chamber from which he hears some laughing. Peeking his head through the curtain, he notices the steward and fan-bearer, Kenamun, sitting in one of the king's chairs while Amenhotep sits on the edge of his bed after recently awakening from a nap. 'Pairy!' calls the king, using the vizier's personal nickname, meaning 'companion'. 'Kenamun was just telling me about the dispute about the boundary marker and the hippo! Won't those two ever stop?'

'I see that Kenamun enjoys listening to my business,' replies Amenemopet half-seriously. Kenamun, too, was a childhood friend of both him and the king so little offence is meant.

'So what's the report?' enquires Amenhotep.

'All is fine in Egypt at the moment,' comes the vizier's reply. 'All is fine. However, shortly we need to walk to the Audience Hall. The treasurer has arranged for a presentation of tribute. Everything is ready when you are.'

Amenemopet knows that, of all the royal activities that take place in the palace, this is Amenhotep's favourite. Often new and sometimes bizarre items would appear but, even if not, the king would take delight in seeing strange animals and the exotic dress of the captives or tribute bearers bringing their gifts.

Even though Amenemopet constructed an elaborate tomb for himself in a hillside on the west bank of Thebes where many wealthy bureaucrats were buried, he would be buried elsewhere. In a gesture of extreme respect, he was ultimately buried in a tomb in the royal cemetery, an honour accorded to few outside the familial circle of the king. In comparison to his originally intended burial place, his tomb in the Valley of the Kings is very simple, composed of a plain shaft and a single undecorated chamber, but it lies in close proximity to the grandiose royal tomb of the ruler he served, Amenhotep II. When discovered in 1906, the tomb was found to have been violently robbed (as were most tombs in the Valley), but the mummy of Amenemopet remained, lying on the floor, along with several objects bearing his name. The author of this book re-excavated the tomb in 2009 and many of the ransacked burial items were still inside.

THE FAN-BEARER
LOOKS ON

The ruler, Aakheperure Amenhotep, strolls across the palace compound to the Audience Hall accompanied by his vizier, Amenemopet. Kenamun, the duly appointed Fan-Bearer on the Right, follows directly behind, keeping perfect pace while expertly shading and cooling his ruler with a large fan composed of exotic wood gilded in gold and bedecked with ostrich plumes. Everything looks typically perfect and worthy of a divine ruler, Kenamun thinks, and is sure to impress even the most spoiled or sceptical of foreign leaders. The exterior gates to the Hall are still closed and a double line of armed soldiers bearing spears and shields begins to form an intimidating corridor leading to it.

Entering the large room, Amenhotep is greeted by the treasurer, Djehutynefer, who understatedly promises an impressive show of newly acquired goods. A dozen scribes sit attentively along two of the walls, their legs crossed and a sheet of papyrus spread across their kilts at the ready. Towards the back of the Audience Hall, a gilded throne sits on an elevated dais, positioned in such a way that a beam of sunlight from a slot-like window would strike the king, giving him an otherworldly glow guaranteed to convince visitors that they are in the presence of divinity. Kenamun follows as the king takes his place and a chamberlain rushes forward to place a footrest beneath his feet, one embellished with the incised depiction of a Nubian and an Asiatic, two categories of Egypt's despised enemies, symbolically trampled whenever Amenhotep takes his seat. Another chamberlain gently places the double crown on his ruler's head before retreating to the wings.

There were several crowns that could be worn by the ruler of Egypt. A red crown which rose to an upward point at the back, represented Lower Egypt, while a crown resembling a white bowling pin symbolized Upper Egypt. Worn together, the double crown reinforced the ever-repeated notion that the king was the Lord of the Two Lands. The ruler might also wear a cloth headdress, with a golden band holding it in place. A special blue crown was often worn while engaged in warfare, and for some public appearances.

Kenamun takes his own place, slightly behind and a little to the right of the throne, gently and rhythmically waving his fan, being careful to avoid the tall crown. Even though they are best friends, it is essential that Kenamun maintains a strictly obsequious demeanour in the presence of Amenhotep when the king is in public and likewise restrain his excitement for what will be taking place in the coming hour. Another fan-bearer takes his place on the left of the king and the cumulative effect projects stunning prestige and power.

Although fan-bearers had been a regular component of the ruler's entourage for centuries, the title 'Fan-Bearer on the Right' first appears during the reign of Amenhotep II. Given the physical closeness of such individuals to the ruler, and their attendance at official occasions, they must have been loyal and highly trusted.

With everything in place, the treasurer, Djehutynefer, asks Amenhotep if he is ready, while Kenamun and his fellow fan-bearer strike an appropriately serious stance. The king nods and the order is given to open the gates and allow a slow, controlled procession to enter the Audience Hall. The treasurer announces each group of representatives who would be allowed to catch a glimpse of the resplendent pharaoh, an awesome if not terrifying sight that would be excitedly shared if or when the foreigners returned home. Looking directly at the ruler or addressing him personally would not be allowed.

FOREIGNERS WERE USUALLY CONSIDERED AGENTS OF CHAOS. FROM LEFT TO RIGHT: NUBIANS, LIBYANS AND ASIATICS, AS DEPICTED IN THE TOMB OF THE RULER, SETI I

First in the Hall is a group of Nubians accompanied by a squad of Egyptian soldiers and a scribe who serves as a translator. 'Behold! Representatives of wretched Nubia!' announces Djehutynefer. Three or four at the front are wearing white kilts and have feathers stuck into their short black hair, and are ornamented with ivory necklaces and earrings. Kenamun, still gently fanning the king, realizes from their attire that they must be chiefs. After approaching the throne, they retreat, bent over in supplication, to the entrance of the Audience Hall behind them, followed by dozens of nearly naked tribute-bearers, sweating under the weight of the baskets and jars perched on their heads. Kenamun is thoroughly enjoying the spectacle from his vantage point.

The traditional enemies of Egypt were known as the Nine Bows. There was little love for the occupants of foreign lands, and their submission and humiliation was constantly reinforced in royal art. Temple walls were embellished with scenes of their death at the hands of the ruler himself, or their submission and humiliation, and the names of vanquished cities and tribes were proudly listed by name. Objects from the virtually intact tomb of the pharaoh, Tutankhamun, symbolically represented the degradation of foreigners, including sandals and a footstool whose use put the enemies literally under the ruler's feet.

Through their translator, the chiefs describe their gifts. First, a number of baskets are placed on the floor in front of the dais and are filled to their rims with pulverized gold from several jars. A few more contain random assortments of gold jewellery no doubt collected from individual Nubians back home. Then a score of bare-chested women are paraded slowly before the throne for consideration as servants or concubines. After examination, each makes a quick exit.

Next come dozens of men carrying over their shoulders cut logs of ebony wood, which are piled neatly off to the side before the bearers turn about and exit. Several beautiful trees are brought in, being supported by horizontal poles, their bases set in dirt-filled baskets, and then several bundles of feathers from exotic birds. And next stacks of panther and cheetah skins along with elephant tusks, each one of them no doubt acquired at great risk to their Nubian hunters.

Thutmose III, father of Amenhotep II, maintained his own botanical garden housing exotic trees and plants from all over Egypt's empire. Depictions of his collection were recorded in one of the chambers he constructed at the expanding Karnak temple complex on the east bank of the Nile.

The parade of exotic goods from Nubia continues. A dozen ostriches march into the room, each restrained by at least one handler. Both their feathers and eggs are valued and, if cared for properly, the birds might survive in the confines of their pens. And then some huge baboons, likewise on leashes, strut forward looking every which way, while each handler has a small monkey on his shoulder. Kenamun hates monkeys of all kinds and sizes, and they seem to hate him, too. Several of them could be seen roaming the palace as Amenhotep finds them amusing and considers them to be his personal pets. The Nubian baboons are allegedly tame, but they are still very unpredictable, often mean and somewhat destructive. 'I bet they've been trained to hate Egyptians!' Kenamun muses.

NUBIAN TRIBUTE-BRINGERS PRESENT A GIRAFFE

Following the monkeys are creatures much more to Kenamun's liking. A pair of baby lions walk side-by-side, looking absolutely noble even while panting in the heat. And then a pair of young giraffes, animals that the Egyptians find interesting, but have a hard time caring for. Directly behind is the last item of Nubian tribute for the month: an adolescent black panther with an embossed leather collar, its sleek fur and yellow eyes drawing a gasp from many of those assembled. Kenamun loves cats of all sizes but is especially fond of the smaller, more domestic varieties. It is easy to be afraid of or annoyed by many of the animals found in Egypt, but cats are different. They could be independent and endearing with the bonus of catching and killing small vermin, and their bites and scratches are rarely fatal.

An appreciation for cats in Egypt is well documented. At least two deities represented felines: the fierce warlike lioness, Sekhmet, and Bastet, who took the form of a small domestic cat, but both were regarded as warlike and protective. Several cat mummies have been discovered in their own wooden coffins, and thousands have been found in a cemetery of votive offerings dedicated to Bastet. Prince Thutmose, a great-grandson of Amenhotep who didn't live to become king, had a beloved pet cat for whom he had a beautiful carved and inscribed limestone coffin made.

After what has seemed like an endless stream of Nubian treasures, a parade of well-ordered Egyptians arrives to remove the tribute. Kenamun sees Amenemopet give Amenhotep a knowing smile. They both love the produce of Nubia. When the Audience Hall is finally cleared, it is time for the next regional group to present their goods. They are representatives of a number of 'vile Asiatic cities, towns and tribes', it is announced, each owing tribute demanded by the invading Egyptians. Amenhotep has no love for any of them; he has seen many Egyptians killed in battle with these very people. A couple of dozen with long hair, beads and colourful kilts and shirts march in and form two lines in front of the throne. 'Place yourselves down before the living god Horus, Aakheperure!' orders Amenemopet, and his words are immediately conveyed via the interpreters. 'Down! Crawl! Stop!' Amenhotep looks down expressionless as one with supreme power might. Kenamun holds back a chuckle while watching the spectacle. After several minutes nervously prone, the chiefs are dismissed with a curt, 'Go home! Tell your people what you have seen in Egypt. Return with fear and respect! Go!' They slowly rise, heads bowed, and back their way out of the room.

Immediately, the Asiatic tribute begins to arrive, and in great quantity. Basket after basket of confiscated or contributed finished gold jewellery is presented, personal items collected to meet their quota. This is followed by a few dozen comely women with long black hair and modest dresses, spinning slowly before the throne before making their exit. A stocky, scraggly Asiatic man marches forth with a black bear on a tether. The bear, moaning in discontent, surely isn't enjoying the experience. Kenamun and Amenhotep's entourage have rarely seen this kind of creature before, and Kenamun finds it fascinating. He recalls similar bears have mauled sailors while being transported, they are expensive to maintain, and their furry coats are unsuitable in Egypt's climate. Nonetheless, they are interesting animals to observe if kept in controlled circumstances.

Kenamun is happy when he sees what is coming next. They will interest Amenhotep more than any of the incredible riches presented so far: horses! The king keeps a stable of the sturdiest and fastest, and enjoys their tenacity when pulling his chariot into battle. There must be a hundred horses coming towards them, each well groomed and many with a feather plume attached to its head. One after the other they slowly parade by the dais. The last dozen or so pull captured chariots with Egyptian handlers in control. Amenhotep would keep and train the best.

'Anything else?' asks the pharaoh expectantly. 'Yes,' answers Djehutynefer. 'A delegation from Keftiu.' Amenhotep has previously told Kenamun that he has no issues with the Keftiu people. They live on the island of Crete in the Great Green, the large sea to the north of Egypt, and trade peacefully with the Egyptians, most of the time. 'Bring them in,' orders the king.

The Keftiu representatives arrive, their physical appearance distinct from the Nubians and Asiatics, as is their dress. Unlike the others, Kenamun notes, they aren't required to grovel, but kneel and bow. Their gifts are mostly in the form of jars containing wine, which are quite welcome. The vizier on behalf of the still-intimidating king sends them on their way and the Hall is once again cleared of goods.

Amenhotep rises from his throne and stretches his legs while the scribes scurry off. 'Are you pleased?' asks Kenamun. Before the ruler can answer, Kenamun offers his own opinion: 'Not bad, but we saw more a couple of months ago. Why didn't the Nubians bring incense? I would rather have incense than another pair of giraffes! And those Syrians; I don't like their beards. Someone should shave them. And where are the Libyans? Have they nothing to offer this time?' Amenhotep just walks away without comment. It has been a splendid exhibition nonetheless.

THE GREAT ROYAL WIFE MAKES DEMANDS

Tiaa sits on her comfortable chair in a pavilion near the Nile, deep in thought while a couple of attendants stand nearby, ready to answer any request. Indeed, there would be some demands, but they would be addressed to her own husband, Amenhotep, Lord of Upper and Lower Egypt, and Son of the Sun. There are a number of items on the agenda including whether or not he views her as a threat to his rule. Amenhotep has continued the erasure of the memory of a female royal predecessor, Hatshepsut, but her reign is yet to be forgotten. There are just too many monuments to her credit including the gleaming obelisks that could be seen at long distances from Karnak. Her statues could be smashed, and her name chiselled off monuments, but there are still too many people alive from her time to wipe away recollections and legends.

As the Great Royal Wife, Tiaa doesn't want to appear to be too ambitious, even if she contemplates doing a few unconventional things. The lesson of Hatshepsut's reign is clear: women should not be the ruler of Egypt, for both traditional and even theological reasons. It is doubtful if it would ever be allowed to happen again and it probably won't, especially given that Tiaa has already given birth to several boys. And unlike some of the kings of the past, Amenhotep has yet to take on any secondary wives. His father Thutmose did, including three foreign women from Syria.

Some Egyptologists have speculated that perhaps Hatshepsut was planning to install her only child, a daughter named Neferure, as her successor. Neferure, however, seems to have disappeared or died while Hatshepsut still reigned, Hatshepsut having effectively grasped the reins of power from Thutmose III while he was still a child. The young prince was more than ready to rule on his own after her death.

As was the tradition, the oldest son still alive at the death of Amenhotep would be the next ruler. Tiaa definitely has her favourite, a congenial fellow named Thutmose who would be the fourth ruler with that name. And she likes the fact that when her husband dies, she would take on the role and title of King's Mother, arguably a role as powerful and influential as Great Royal Wife. Tiaa knows that all too well as her still-living mother-in-law, Merytre-Hatshepsut, is domineering and has much too much sway over her son. Among other things, she has demanded a tomb for herself in the royal cemetery in a location close to her son's burial. Tiaa feels she should have the same.

There are suggestions that there might have been some sort of palace intrigue involving the succession of Thutmose IV to the throne. A large stele erected at the Great Sphinx in Giza bears a text that goes well out of its way to legitimize his reign, and includes the story of the prince being contacted by the Sphinx as a god in a dream. If he were to free the Sphinx from the sand which buried him, he would become ruler of Egypt. Some Egyptologists find such a curious proclamation of legitimacy somewhat suspicious in its motivation.

When Tiaa made enquiries to some of the overseers working on Amenhotep's tomb, they revealed that some royal women had tombs in remote cliffs south of the royal cemetery. They had been constructed by tunnelling into the rock far off the ground to thwart their tampering by any who might wish to loot them. She now knows that a tomb was constructed for Hatshepsut before she became ruler and another for her daughter Neferure, and yet another for all three of Thutmose's Syrian wives. Such a remote location far from her husband's tomb simply would not do, concludes Tiaa.

Apart from Hatshepsut, there were very few women who served as ruler of ancient Egypt during its 3000 years of history. Clues exist that an early queen of Egypt, Meryt-Neith, might have had that role but her name is not mentioned in the ancient lists of kings (but then again, neither is that of the well-attested Hatshepsut). Another woman, Nitocris of the Sixth Dynasty, is listed, but there is no outside physical evidence for her existence. Sobeknefru apparently ruled for about six years during the Twelfth Dynasty. There was Hatshepsut during the Eighteenth Dynasty, of course, but some have argued that a later queen of the same era, Nefertiti, became ruler at the death of her controversial husband, Akhenaten. Another woman, Twosret, reigned for perhaps two years on her own during the chaotic end of the Nineteenth Dynasty. And then there was the famed Cleopatra a thousand years later. Despite her reputation as an Egyptian queen, she was actually a Greek queen of Egypt who presided over the end of 300 years of Greek rule during the expansion of the Roman Empire.

Living a pampered life with few active responsibilities other than bearing children mostly looked after by others, and making appearances with Amenhotep on occasion, there is plenty of time for Tiaa to think about things such as tombs. Or how Amenhotep is often off doing physically strenuous, if not dangerous, things for his own amusement, or to demonstrate his divine abilities and fitness to the adoring masses. She especially deplores the archery from a moving chariot and she thinks that running is silly. Rowing, though, is fun to watch, especially from a luxurious shaded dais on the river's edge while cool breezes blow. She is, though, yet to be convinced of the legend of her husband's super-human prowess with an oar, nor all of his outrageous heroics as reported in battlefield legends and on temple walls.

Many of Egypt's rulers maintained 'harems', a facility where royal women and children could live and be attended by a contingent of obliging servants. During the reign of Rameses III, a conspiracy was plotted by one of his lesser wives who wanted to kill him in order to place her own favourite son on the throne, and the king's mummy seems to indicate they were successful. The details that describe the charges and verdicts against the conspirators have survived on papyrus documents. Although in most cases the specifics of the punishments are not described, they must have been severe, and some of the guilty were allowed to take their own lives.

TIAA, THE ROYAL WIFE OF AMENHOTEP II

Another thing that annoys Tiaa is Amenhotep's pets. There are a number of overly well-fed and well-groomed hunting hounds that are sleek and eager to please. Occasionally, Amenhotep would allow them into the royal residency where they would sprint about the palace to the delight of their master. And even when they are outside, one would often hear their yipping in the distance. And then there are the monkeys. Tiaa does not care the least bit for them nor understand their attraction, and to let them roam about the palace compound? More than once she had insisted that her husband rid himself of his unpredictable and frisky companions but to no avail. At times she would visit another palace without him, but when she returned, the pets would always still be here, and often there were additions to the collection.

Although she has been away from the palace for most of the day, Tiaa knows what went on earlier. It was yet another grandiose presentation of tribute by foreigners. She finds this sort of display rather distasteful with their exceptional amount of noise, sweat and unusual odours, all influenced by a tinge of fear at being in the presence of Egypt's ruler and his intimidating soldiers and bureaucrats. She does, however, appreciate some of the humbly presented luxury items, and when all had cleared out of the residence, Amenhotep would let her plough through the baskets of foreign jewellery to select anything she liked.

A messenger arrives to inform the queen that her husband would be coming by soon. Just a few minutes later, the sound of laughing announces his arrival. Amenhotep looks delighted as does his vizier, Amenemopet, and his close friend, Kenamun. 'He sees more of them than he does me!' she thinks. Following the three men are several soldiers tending leashes. Just as Tiaa dreaded, there are more animals. 'Look, Tiaa!' said Amenhotep by way of greeting. 'A bear from Syria! Make him stand on his back legs,' commands the king. One of the soldiers slaps the bear with a stick and the animal stands tall for a few moments before returning to his natural stance. Tiaa had seen it all before and isn't impressed.

Baby giraffes follow, which Tiaa feels are like so many other animals: often cute when small but lose much of their appeal when they become adults. Thus far, the small menagerie is obnoxious yet tolerable but, soon enough, the dreaded monkeys make their appearance. Even with leashes, their incessant leaping and quick motions, and endless chattering, provide no end of annoyance.

Three small undecorated tombs in the Valley of the Kings remain somewhat of a puzzle to archaeologists. Located close to the tomb of Amenhotep II, each contained the mummies of monkeys and, in one case, a dog as well. The sharp canine teeth of some of the animals had been removed, perhaps to make them safer in the company of humans. Their proximity to Amenhotep's tomb suggests a connection. Could they have been his pets? Or those of another ruler? Or could they serve some sort of ritual purpose?

Amenhotep could read the irritation on his queen's face. 'Today's contributions were excellent! And you should see the jewellery. Come back to the palace and take a look!'

'I'd like to have a few words alone with you first,' replies Tiaa.

Amenhotep orders the others to take the animals away and, once they are outside of hearing range, Tiaa begins her short list of demands.

'First, I want a tomb in the royal cemetery. I don't wish to be interred in some horrible remote cliff near your father's many women.'

Amenhotep appears to think for a moment but then agrees without too much hesitation. 'I can arrange for that. It will be suitable, but don't expect it to be grandiose like mine. I am the Living Horus, remember?'

Next, Tiaa once again insists on assurance that she would remain the sole wife and not have competition with other lesser queens, nor have to deal with offspring produced by them. Nor does she want him to receive gifts of foreign princesses as his father did. Nor does she want him associating with the dozens of naked women presented to him during the tribute presentations. She wants to be taken care of, too.

She holds her breath for her husband's response. Thankfully, Amenhotep offers his promise that one queen will be sufficient. 'You are a great queen and a great royal wife and I can imagine no other. I will look after you.'

With that, the two embrace, Tiaa reassured he doesn't view her as another potential female usurper, as demanding as she knew she occasionally could be. That said, she couldn't resist whispering one more thing into her husband's ear: 'Get rid of the monkeys!'

Tiaa did indeed receive a burial in the New Kingdom royal cemetery known as the 'Valley of the Kings'. It consisted of a couple of sets of stairs and corridors leading to a chamber. Its walls were undecorated, which was typical of those tombs in the Valley that didn't belong to the ruler himself. Archaeologists found the tomb robbed and damaged, but enough traces of burial goods survived to ascertain that the tomb did in fact belong to Tiaa.

10TH HOUR OF THE DAY
(15.00–16.00)

THE PROFESSIONAL MOURNER WAILS YET AGAIN

I am with the mourners [and with] the women who tear out their hair and make lament for Osiris ... proving true the words of Osiris before his enemies.

The Papyrus of Ani

'Muss up your hair some more,' demands Henutnofret, 'you don't look sorrowful enough. And take off that dress and put this on,' she adds as she tosses a filthy kilt at her daughter. Henti slips out of her clean outfit and, like Henutnofret, winds a dirty sheet of linen around her waist. Bare from the waist up, they rubbed white dust on their chests and prepared to leave.

'I hate this work,' complains Henti, 'it makes me feel sad and awkward. And look how I'm dressed or, should I say, not dressed.'

'Maybe if you feel sad, you'll look sad, which is what we want. And your dress? You wear almost nothing when you dance at those parties!'

'That's different, and, in fact, I hope we're done with all of this quickly, because I'm dancing at Userhet's banquet this evening.'

Henutnofret and Henti are professional mourners employed to wail and imitate extreme grief during the funerary rites associated with interments. Today, Ipi was being buried. Perhaps the most disliked man in Thebes, he had, however, a handful of influential friends and was very wealthy – enough to have a tomb situated among those of the elite bureaucrats. Not only did he have a bad reputation in general, his own family utterly detested him, especially his wife, Baketamun. Ipi had been perpetually drunk and enjoyed employing women for 'special favours', but for all of his wealth, he was cheap and shared little. Henutnofret knew that Henti had danced at one of Ipi's parties and not only would the overseer not leave her alone (at the expense of paying attention to his guests), he had also paid her only half of what was promised.

The mummified body had been delivered to Ipi's villa in the morning and was joined by his coffin and a growing assemblage of funerary goods, as well as some food. As Henutnofret and Henti arrive, just about everything is ready for the river crossing to the western side. Hapuneseb the embalmer is present, as well as a couple of priests to perform the rituals, along with dozens of men to carry and haul everything to the tomb. Baketamun stands apart from the others, including her husband's few friends, whom, Henutnofret can see, she also despises. The deceased's children refused to attend. This would be considered a shocking breach of normal decorum, because the eldest son is expected to act the role of a mortuary priest, but no one can blame him given his father's reputation. Fortunately, one of the other priests in attendance has been engaged to perform that function.

The coffin is placed on a special funerary sledge with a wooden canopy provided by the embalmer along with another to carry a chest containing the four jars holding Ipi's entrails. When Hapuneseb gives the word, all line up and the procession begins with several men pulling the sledges and others hoisting a selection of furniture and boxes on their shoulders. The priests lead the way followed by Baketamun and Ipi's friends, the procession of items, and lastly, Henutnofret and Henti. 'Make it look real, even if it is for Ipi,' advises Henutnofret, hoping that the notoriously cheap Baketamun will pay them both the full amount.

The shrieking and faux-grief attract the attention of those along the way, and the procession pauses for a few minutes to load everything on to the boats. Henti and Henutnofret sit silently as the river is crossed but resume the wailing as soon as they disembark on the other side. The road to the hillsides containing the elite cemeteries is both familiar and long, and there are a few short stops along the way to give the bearers and pullers a rest. The short breaks are a good opportunity for the mourners to show their 'anguish' by crouching down with their heads shaking in the dust and sobbing wildly. Henutnofret knows it is clear to everyone that the mourners are paid; not even Ipi's friends have reason to cry for him. Unlike the coffin and many of the other items, wailing women are very inexpensive. Even so, Henutnofret has heard that Baketamun has spent as little as possible. The minimum of useful household goods would make it to the burial, and few provisions were to be sealed into the tomb.

A friend who decorates tombs had told Henutnofret that, several years previously, Ipi, famed for his meanness, had nonetheless commissioned a tomb among those of the Theban high officials. He said it was of the kind not unusual these days – it would have a courtyard in front of a chapel carved into the limestone hillside. The chapel would consist of a doorway opening into a narrow room, which extended to both the left and right. Beyond would be another rectangular chamber. Ipi himself would be buried in a subterranean chamber in the courtyard,

A FUNERAL ATTENDED BY PRIESTS, THE DECEASED IN HIS COFFIN,
AND A COUPLE OF WAILING PROFESSIONAL MOURNERS, AS DEPICTED IN
A BOOK OF THE DEAD BELONGING TO HUNEFER

accessible by a shaft that could be filled in and thus sealed.

Her friend had laughed when he said that Ipi had made sure that his chapel, which would allow for him to be remembered with visits by family and friends, was beautifully painted on plastered walls with appropriate scenes to sustain him in the Afterlife; Ipi must have known that, in reality, few would care once he had passed on. Apart from depicting some of the highlights of his life, including a couple of encounters with Amenhotep, the walls were covered with images of Ipi as strong, handsome and fit, sitting in front of tables piled high with the best food Egypt had to offer. And if pictures weren't enough, accompanying inscriptions made it clear that not only was Ipi an important figure during his lifetime and beyond, but he would be well provisioned whether or not anyone cared.

The ancient Egyptians attributed a kind of supernatural reality to words written or uttered, or depicted in art. Painted scenes in many elite tombs portrayed an idealized Afterlife including offerings of provisions, thereby sustaining or enhancing the necessities of the deceased.

Henutnofret, Henti and the rest of the procession eventually arrived at the courtyard of Ipi's tomb, its chapel only having been finished during the period of mummification. Henutnofret sees that the courtyard itself is plastered white, as is the chapel's doorway above which are two rows of discs, each with a hieroglyphic inscription bearing Ipi's name and titles. The discs are cone-shaped, having been inserted into mortar. In the middle of the courtyard is a deep shaft and all the grave goods are set aside nearby.

Egyptian 'funerary cones' have been found in the thousands, representing hundreds of different officials, especially during the New Kingdom. As the facades of tomb chapels collapsed over the years, the cones fell to the ground and, being portable, they have been collected and sold by antiquities dealers. The exact purpose of the cones is still debated. Interestingly, there are names on some individual cones that are not associated with known tombs, thus suggesting there are many burials in the elite cemeteries yet to be found.

The functionaries and the bearers remove the mummified and wrapped body of Ipi from his coffin and place it in an upright position in front of the chapel entrance. Henutnofret watches as the lector priest steps forward with his scroll and begins reading the incantations. The *sem*-priest, who is practised in the mortuary arts and impressively dressed in pure white garments with a leopard skin draped over his shoulder, then comes forward. His presence is most important as he would direct the purification rituals and 'Opening of the Mouth Ceremony', which would reanimate Ipi's spirit and re-establish his vital functions.

Touching the mummy's mouth with an adze, and then a chisel and other prying tools, the *sem*-priest recites the appropriate spells. From around the corner comes a man with a just-severed cow leg – Henutnofret is sure that it is still twitching a bit – and this, too, is presented to the mummy. The slaughtered animal would be a delicious addition to the memorial feast to follow, and the leftovers would be good payment to the priests and the others participating. All the while, Henutnofret and Henti continue to alternate between whimpering and sobbing with the occasional spontaneous shriek thrown in for good measure.

While performing her wailing duties, Henutnofret would often reflect on the journey that her mourning accompanied. Ipi would now be on his way to the Afterlife and would have quite a perilous excursion to survive on his way to Judgement, which itself could be a nervous ordeal. Henutnofret had already noticed a scroll resting in a jar standing among all the rest of the burial equipment. The papyrus would be a copy of 'The Book of the Dead', which would provide Ipi with instructions to help him reach a successful conclusion to his journey. Judging by Ipi's reputation for frugality, he had probably bought the scroll for a bargain. If so, the writing would probably be rife with mistakes, perhaps just the effort of a scribal student wanting some practice. Sometimes the name of another dead man would simply have been scraped out and replaced.

Travelling through the dark scary Underworld with its unsavoury inhabitants was an ordeal enough, and the right knowledge and spells were necessary to overcome the obstacles. The Judgement Hall, though, was where Ipi's ultimate eternal fate would be decided. There he would find Osiris, god of the dead, sitting on his throne with his two protective sisters, Isis and Nephthys, standing behind. Forty-two assessor-gods would also be present and would ask him if he had committed various wrongdoings while alive. One always denies each proposed wrongdoing. Ultimately, Ipi's heart would be weighed against the feather of *maat*, representing truth, on a scale overseen by Anubis with Thoth recording the proceedings. The heart and *maat* needed to balance or the consequences would be truly dire. Eagerly waiting nearby would be a demonic composite creature, Ammut, the 'devourer of the dead', with the head of a crocodile, the body of a leopard and the hind legs of a hippo. Should the life of the judged be found woefully flawed, his heart would be fed to the creature and the deceased therefore passed into non-existence. There would be no pleasant Afterlife for the wicked.

The Book of the Dead contains the 'Negative Confession' or 'Declarations of Innocence' in which the assessor gods interrogate the deceased. Here is a sample of the deceased's denial of wrongdoing:

I have not committed sin.

I have not committed robbery with violence.

I have not stolen.

I have not slain men and women.

I have not stolen grain.

I have not purloined offerings.

I have not stolen the property of god.

I have not uttered lies.

I have not uttered curses.

I have not attacked any man.

I am not a man of deceit.

I have not stolen cultivated land.

I have not been an eavesdropper.

I have not slandered.

I have not blasphemed.

I am not a man of violence.

I have not stirred up strife.

I have wronged none, I have done no evil.

THE BOOK OF THE DEAD OF ANI

⟵————————————————————⟶

The various rites are now heading towards their conclusion, so a couple of porters climb down the burial shaft by means of small toeholds carved into its side. With the mummy back in its place, the coffin is lowered down with ropes to be received by the men below. Next to follow is the canopic box containing Ipi's organs, and then some furniture, chests of clothing, some baskets of food and some tall wine jars. And a small box containing little wooden figures bearing tools, *shabtis*, which will function as Ipi's servants. Henutnofret notices that nothing particularly valuable is handed down the shaft; Baketamun has clearly seen to that. Finally, the jar containing the Book of the Dead is placed next to the head of the coffin. The workers down below leave the chamber and close up its entrance with stones before climbing to the surface.

Henutnofret and Henti let out a few more squeals when the food for the funerary feast is spread out; they may be the only genuine outbursts of emotion during the entire day. Meat, fruit and wine in abundance. 'Thank you, Ipi,' mutters Henutnofret as she stuffs herself. Although spoken somewhat insincerely, it was probably the nicest thing anyone had said to the now dead Ipi in years.

11TH HOUR OF THE DAY
(16.00–17.00)

THE ARCHITECT
INSPECTS A ROYAL
TOMB

I inspected the cliff-tomb of his majesty alone, no one seeing, no one hearing.

INSCRIPTION FROM THE TOMB OF THE ARCHITECT INENI

It is a hot day as Neswy the architect trudges along the mountain trail, a journey he has been making every few days over the last several years; a journey that he feels he could make in his sleep. He certainly wouldn't want to do so as the path comes close to the edge of vertical cliffs dropping down to the plains on the west bank of Thebes. Down below he can see the memorial temples of the first Amenhotep and the three rulers named Thutmose, and quite prominently, the enormous temples dedicated to Hatshepsut and a ruler from a much earlier time, Montuhotep. He can see a number of attending priests coming and going from the various structures and there is much activity surrounding the construction of the present ruler's own memorial temple. Across the river, the Karnak temple is plainly visible with its obelisks shining brilliantly in the intense sun.

Neswy is on his way to what is certainly one of the most exclusive and secretive places in the land: the royal cemetery of the god-kings. Egypt's last several rulers are buried here, as would be the second Amenhotep. It is a remote desert valley, secluded from the public, who hopefully don't know of its existence. Rising above is a mountain that resembles a great natural pyramid, something that reminds Neswy of the fate of previous royal burial places.

Neswy had more than once travelled north to Memphis and, along the way, he could see the numerous pyramids built of stone or, in some cases, mud-brick. Some were truly massive and could be seen from miles away with their white, gleaming limestone surfaces. Built as the final resting places of the pharaohs from years long past, they were truly spectacular but as Neswy had been informed, they were proving utterly inadequate in protecting their

A DEPICTION OF AMENHOTEP II WITH THE GOD ANUBIS IN THE
BURIAL CHAMBER OF HIS TOMB IN THE VALLEY OF THE KINGS

occupants. Visible to all, the pyramids stood like shining, inviting beacons to tempt any industrious robber with high ambitions. Beginning with the first Thutmose, the tombs of Egypt's rulers would no longer be on public display.

In searching for a good location for the royals' final resting places, those who had explored the desert canyons in the west where the sun sets in the land of the dead had several criteria to fulfil, including remoteness, good quality rock suitable for the building of a royal tomb, reasonable proximity to workers and an easily guardable position. One particular ravine fitted the bill, which had a pyramid-shaped mountain rising directly above, providing suitable symbolic value for all the tombs below. It was the perfect spot.

Neswy is the architect appointed with the serious task of supervising the building of Amenhotep's eternal resting place among his royal predecessors. It is a task with which he already has much experience, having been involved in the construction of the previous ruler's tomb. Building the new tomb is quite a process, which has thus far been underway for almost ten years. Hopefully it would be finished before Amenhotep flew away to the next horizon.

The trail to the valley begins at a very special village where Neswy lived, one unlike any other found in Egypt. It is composed of workers and artisans whose primary job is to carry out the construction of the royal tombs. With a population of dozens including family members, the village is located close to the cliffs, well away from the general populace and close enough to the tombs so that they can hike to work as often as necessary. As such, the village needs to be independently supplied with not only the tools necessary to do the work, but a lot of the essentials of daily life including water. The work is typically difficult and strenuous, but the workmen get the last two days off each ten-day week of the Egyptian calendar.

The village of workmen for the royal tombs is known today by its Arabic name, Deir el-Medina. It has been excavated and studied by archaeologists for over a hundred years. Having been abandoned at the end of the New Kingdom, and situated in a dry desert environment, it survived well preserved, providing scholars with an extraordinary look at daily life from that time, although admittedly from an atypical settlement. With skills honed from constructing royal tombs, some of the residents of the workmen's village built their own tombs in the vicinity of their homes. Although generally small, they were usually beautifully decorated, and some have been found with their contents intact.

Neswy resides in the village and finds life there, at times, stifling. It is, in fact, physically restrictive and not everyone gets along. There are arguments, as expected in any community, and occasional disputes about compensation or the distribution of goods needed to sustain the workers.

It is also an environment in which it is very easy for marital scandals and legal disputes to go public quickly. And if one wants to get away for an hour or two, there aren't too many options. Still, the village is well located. And it is a privilege to be there among those trusted and skilled enough to work on royal tombs, Neswy would attempt to convince himself after a bad day, an attitude he tries to share with his underlings.

Eventually Neswy reaches a low spot on the trail, encountering a small cluster of stone huts suitable for both guardians of the tomb and workmen. With cool winds blowing through, they offer an often pleasant place to rest or even spend the night if one did not wish to return to the confines and drama of the village. Just past the huts, the trail drops diagonally downward to reach the valley floor. Continuing on and rounding a small hill, the workmen come into view on an opposite slope.

The first tombs in this, the Valley of the Kings, are situated away from the valley's floor and directly under water courses that can become active during rainfall. They are natural features that provide a good starting place for the building of tombs, and debris brought down during the occasional rain might serve to further hide the finished and sealed tomb. Placing a tomb down below on the flat valley bed could expose it to wild flash floods that could obliterate anything in their path.

The past pharaoh, the third Thutmose, situated his tomb

high up in the side of one of the valley's cliffs, an unlikely but easily protected location. Its design was impressive. Carved into the limestone, it began with a steep, straight descent down sets of stairs and sloping corridors. The slope ended at a deep pit, which could serve as protection for the workmen in the event of unexpected flooding, and also an obstacle to thwart robbers. Across the pit was the entrance to one corner of a small antechamber-like room featuring a couple of pillars. Here one must take a sharp turn to the left to continue on. The antechamber's walls were decorated with depictions of hundreds of beings noted in the *Amduat* – the ancient text reserved for royal burials, which describes the deceased ruler's journey with the sun through the perilous twelve hours of the Underworld's night to be again reborn with the sun.

Another set of stairs led down to the burial chamber, which featured two pillars and four storerooms. The chamber itself was extraordinary, with its oval shape representing a cartouche, an elongated version of the Egyptian symbol for eternity: a circle of rope tied into a continuous loop. Near the back was the sarcophagus of the king himself. Made from a single chunk of yellow quartzite with an accompanying lid, it too resembled a cartouche. The walls were decorated with freely drawn sections of the *Amduat* and its ceiling was painted to represent a starry sky. The entire tomb was stunning, it being an original design with no other royal burial like it. Amenhotep wants one very similar.

By the end of the New Kingdom, the majority of tombs in the royal cemetery had been robbed and the Valley of the Kings would soon be abandoned. Not long afterwards, a cadre of priests examined each tomb and collected the ravaged mummies which were then rewrapped and stored in a couple of secret caches to protect them from further plundering. The tomb of Amenhotep II was used for one such cache, and along with the ruler himself, sixteen other mummies were found within.

Neswy approaches the workmen, many of whom are busy hauling out basket after basket of limestone chips produced from the subterranean construction. At the sight of Neswy, they pick up speed to an unsustainable rate in order to impress. One man runs down into the tomb to fetch Gua, the supervisor, who minutes later emerges up the stairs, coughing and white with dust. The two greet each other warmly and Neswy asks how the project is coming along as he removes and unrolls a papyrus scroll from a satchel over his shoulder, revealing the tomb's plan. The diagram looks nearly identical to the layout of the third Thutmose's tomb but with straighter features and a burial chamber with straight walls and six pillars. Gua points to the final set of steps. 'We're here, and soon we will be forming the jambs for the burial chamber. Let's hope that our ruler lives long enough to see it all finished.' Neswy agrees.

The Valley of the Kings was used as a royal cemetery for most of the New Kingdom, about five hundred years. A tomb is known for nearly every ruler of the era but two have yet to be found or identified: those of Thutmose II and Rameses X. The two might have been interred in known tombs but, having left no surviving traces, the possibility exists that their burials have yet to be found. Scattered among the grandiose royal tombs, there are also a few dozen smaller undecorated tombs that belonged to other royal family members or special associates including Amenemopet, Amenhotep II's vizier.

Gua has his own copy of the tomb's plan; it was carefully drawn on a large flat flake of limestone, and Neswy knows that he keeps it in the tomb and consults it regularly. Gua supervises two groups of carvers, one for each side of a tomb's corridors or features. When a new section is started, a tunnel is dug, and a straight line inked down the centre. The two crews could then carve away in each direction to produce symmetrical features. It isn't all that difficult, but it requires regular vigilance to keep everything in order.

'Would you like to take a look?' asks Gua. Despite his position, Neswy really doesn't like descending into a tomb while it is under construction. The air is always full of choking dust and produces a haze that restricts vision. He prefers to visit very early or on the days when the workmen are resting and the interior chambers readily inspected.

'No, perhaps next time. Do you need anything?' asks the architect, even though supplies aren't part of his official job.

He watches Gua think for a moment. 'Yes, soon we'll need a resupply of lamp wicks and oil. And some more lamps as well. And the men want more water and some linen rags to clean themselves. And more beer.'

'Anything else?' asks Neswy.

'Yes, they need more chisels and wooden mallets,' explains Gua as he points to a large basket full of bent and dull copper tools and broken chunks of wood.

'Anything else?'

'The guards tell me they don't like the food and there isn't enough of it.'

'More?'

'Yes. We want two of the donkeys replaced. They complain too much. Too much noise, especially at night.'

Neswy decides to stop asking questions. Instead, he removes the small sack slung over his shoulder and takes out his scribal kit. After mixing up some black ink on his palette with a dab of water, he picks up a small flake of limestone and makes notes. 'Lamps, wicks and oil, chisels and mallets, beer, good food. I'll take care of this,' he promises Gua as he packed up his items to leave. 'I'll be back in a few days.'

Crossing the valley to hike the trail back to the village, he hears Gua's voice echoing across the way: 'And don't forget what I said about those donkeys!'

THE VALLEY OF THE KINGS TODAY WITH THE
ENTRANCE TO THE TOMB OF AMENHOTEP II

Egyptologists have benefited greatly from the many hundreds
of ostraca – notes written on scraps of broken pottery or flakes
of stone – that have survived from both Deir el-Medina and
the Valley of the Kings. The ostraca provide an unparalleled
look at daily life in the village, but also many of the details
involved in the construction of the royal tombs.

12TH HOUR OF THE DAY
(17.00–18.00)

THE CARPENTER
FINISHES A COFFIN

It is the twelfth hour of the day when Nebseni and his helpers set down yet another finished coffin among half a dozen others in the covered area of the workshop. For whatever reason, there had been a spate of deaths of well-off people in the last few months and so the craftsmen had been especially busy. There had been a drowning, a murder, and several others had contracted diseases that the physicians couldn't cure. And then there was Ipi who fell off a wall only to be found a few days later. Nebseni, as a master carpenter, had just that morning delivered his coffin to his widow, Baketamun, at their impressive villa. A couple of months previously, she had appeared at Nebseni's workshop just a few days after her husband's death to order up a 'box of life'. He had already heard from the embalmers that she would demand nothing but the worst.

Nebseni had answered her request by proclaiming that all of his work was excellent even though it came in a variety of price ranges, from simple coffins with a minimum of embellishment to those with gold-gilded faces and hands and beautiful stone inlays. As predicted, she asked for the cheapest. 'Cheap like him,' she clarified as she tried to negotiate the cost downward; an effort that failed. 'It will be less expensive but nice, and delivered to your home in time for his burial,' promised the carpenter.

The solution to the problem had been simple. Ipi would receive a recycled coffin, the family who had originally requested it having refused to pay for it after it was finished. It then became mostly a matter of simply repainting the few lines of text over those noting the name of the other man.

Nebseni has a good reputation in the coffin-making business and today he is concentrating on fulfilling as many commissions for the burials to come as possible. He also is known for making expensive, beautifully constructed furniture for the home or tomb of those able to afford it. He isn't greedy but, as a craftsman with high standards, he only wanted to work with the best materials. Unfortunately, trees do not grow in thick forests in Egypt. And they tend to be narrow and scraggly, making it difficult to extract wooden planks from them of any great size. There are lots of acacia trees along with tamarisks and sycamore-fig, too, and although usable, none are ideal for high quality manufacturing. For that, the finer wood would need to be imported.

The best source is a good distance from Egypt but worth the travel. In lands out on the eastern coast of the Great Green and inland from the area of Byblos (Lebanon), there are vast cedar and other conifer groves providing the ideal wood for the best items. Expeditions by ship to that region have been taking place for a thousand years with crews armed with axes, axe-sharpeners and ropes. After the trees are felled, the limbs are cut off and trimmed to be kept, and the great trunks dragged to the harbour. Those that can't be cut into logs or other smaller pieces on the spot could be towed floating behind the boats back to Egypt for further processing and distribution.

⟵————————————————————————⟶

In 1954, a large sealed pit was accidentally discovered at the base of the Great Pyramid in Giza. When opened, it was found to contain the dismantled pieces of a perfectly preserved ancient ship made from imported cedar and dating back to the time of the ruler, Khufu (*c*. 2600 BC). The boat might have been buried as a part of Khufu's funerary assemblage and/or actually used to convey his body down the Nile to his burial site. The boat was 43.4 metres in length and included a cabin and long oars and its planks were held in place by ropes, which also survived well. It took years for conservators to put it all back together and today it can be viewed in a museum built over its site of discovery. An adjacent pit was also opened but the boat within was in much poorer shape, cracks having exposed it to the elements.

←——————————————————————————→

Nebseni had once worked in a shipyard where he learned a lot about shaping and sizing planks to construct hulls. Working with scraps and fragments of all sizes, he became an expert at cutting and drilling – and tying knots as well. It all helped out when he joined a carpentry shop owned by an uncle and learned the finer arts of making furniture and coffins. When the uncle died, Nebseni became the boss and owner, supervising a dozen craftsmen of varying experience. The workshop itself consists of a spacious walled courtyard where most of the work takes place, and a covered area with a couple of rooms to store tools and finished items.

When a project is requested, there is the matter of selecting available wood. The finest is the imported cedar with its wide planks and pleasant aroma, or else ebony. The latter is brought from foreign lands far to the south and is valued for its dark colour, strength and durability.

Otherwise, there are the usual Egyptian options. The corners of the courtyard contain piles of scraps from other projects along with stacks of cut logs from various trees. In the centre is the cutting area where logs could be set on end and lashed to a sturdy post. Using saws, planks could be produced by cutting down from the top to the base.

A CARPENTER TRIMS WOOD

Nebseni and his craftsmen are experts at finding just the right planks and scraps to create any individual coffin or piece of furniture. Two irregular pieces of wood could be made to match each other using adzes and chisels. The adzes of various sizes consist of metal blades lashed with leather bindings to a wooden handle, which resembles a hoe; a large one could be swung for rough hacking while smaller ones are capable of delicate shaping. Their blades require regular sharpening, as do the chisels. Matched pairs of wood pieces could be joined and held together via mortise and tenon, dovetail joints or hard wooden pegs. The surfaces could be smoothed by hand with a sandstone block to produce a uniform surface. Any irregularities or blemishes in the material could be relieved by a thick or thin coat of gypsum plaster which could be beautifully painted.

Boxes, beds and chairs are the most popular kinds of domestic furniture ordered. Being rectangular, the boxes are relatively easy although a mix of wood such as ebony and cedar would require more care. If the customer wants inlays, the decoration might take some time, especially if it involves items such as ivory derived from hippo teeth or imported elephant tusks. The lids could vary considerably, from one that is flat, to others that give a roofed or curved effect. Most contained at least one mushroom-shaped knob on top and optionally another in front if the chest is to be sealed shut with a knotted cord and stamped clay.

Chairs could be a bit more complex and have various options for customization. Nebseni always requests information on the size of the individual for whom the object is intended. There is no use wasting time constructing a fine piece of furniture for an adult if it is meant for a child, or a dainty seat to be used in the home of a large and heavy man. Like everything else, the chairs could be simple or elaborate. The seat itself could be of solid wood or of plaited reeds, and the possibilities for decoration are endless. Very popular are chair legs ending in carved representations of animal feet, usually those of a bull or lion.

The artisans at Nebseni's workshop are well aware of some of the special advantages that they have over the average working-class Egyptian, most of whom have little if any furniture in their own homes and sleep on mats or thin mattresses. And when they sit, they either squat or set themselves down on the floor or ground. Nebseni's men could do much of their work from the practical comfort of short stools, which facilitate their ability to work, and if there are unwanted scraps, and the rare free moment, the boss would allow his crew to create items for their own homes. It would be good to be married to such a craftsman!

Nebseni looks at beds as another kind of luxury almost in the form of an elongated chair complete with four legs but with a place to lie. Typically they are low to the ground but served well their purpose of avoiding hard surfaces and nocturnal vermin which might traipse across the floor (and sleepers) at night.

Although Nebseni loves to make household furniture best, funerary goods are becoming much of his business.

A lot of his regular products, including chairs and beds, are also specifically created for burial, especially if the family don't want to give away their still-useful items to be placed in a sealed tomb, thereby requiring purchase of new items. The master carpenter doesn't care how or where his creations are used; each piece would be good even if, like Ipi's wife, the customer wanted a minimalistic product.

Coffins require special care. Given their importance in holding the deceased's remains, their spiritual survival might partially depend on the survival of their physical mummy. Protective gods and goddesses decorating their surfaces are to guard the coffin's occupant and this is not to be taken lightly.

MAKING A COFFIN FROM CUTTING THE PLANKS TO ITS COMPLETED STATE

Nebseni discourages joking in his workshop regarding anything dealing with coffins, no matter the reputation or looks of the intended occupant. When it came to Ipi, the workers had a hard time restraining themselves.

'I saw Ipi,' declared one of the junior carpenters, 'and he didn't look anything like what's on the lid!'

'I've seen him, too!' chimed another. 'He'll never fit into that coffin unless they cut him in half!'

'Enough! Have some respect!' yelled kind-hearted Nebseni, who knew very well that they were correct. Ipi's wife wanted the cheapest coffin for her detested husband, but it would be the embalmer's problem to squeeze him in.

Before beginning work, the estimated size of a finished mummy would be gathered from the embalmers who had, literally, first-hand knowledge of the corpse. Planks of the proper size and quality would be selected, or produced if needed. Wood from the sycamore-fig is popular and cedar might be used for the best. Unlike most of the coffins in eras past, relatively simple rectangular boxes are not the current trend. Instead, the coffin would resemble, more or less, a human body with a head and shoulders and tapering at the foot end. The end result would be an idealized vision of the deceased, no matter how old or ugly, to carry them towards the anticipated Afterlife.

Some of the earliest known Egyptian religious texts come from inscriptions on the stone walls of the later pyramids of the Old Kingdom (c. 2700 to 2200 BC). Very esoteric in nature, including rituals, hymns, protective incantations and descriptions of the king's heavenly ascension, they were reserved for the god-kings, and at the end of the Old Kingdom, also for queens. During the Middle Kingdom, versions of these 'Pyramid Texts', supplemented with further material, were painted on the inside surfaces of coffins belonging to elite commoners. Not surprisingly, Egyptologists refer to these as the 'Coffin Texts'. Some coffins of this period included beautifully painted depictions of offerings presented to the deceased. The texts and paintings together transformed a rectangular coffin into what resembled a tomb, in and of itself. The coffins, though, were put into their tombs as intended.

←——————————————————————————→

These sorts of coffins would require a lot of work, even given the seventy days or so needed for the mummification process. With shoulders curved and the head-end crowned, there would be a lot of shaping involved in both the box portion and the lid. Nebseni's men are certainly up to the task but it is time-consuming. Matching the lid and box would require care to produce a perfect fit. The lid would feature a delicate portrait of the deceased including the face and hands. These would be carved separately to be pinned into the lid and covered with a thin layer of gypsum for painting or gilding in gold. The popular trend also requires that much of the rest of the coffin is covered with a black resin. Down the middle of the coffin's lid and along the sides of the box would be painted lines of funerary texts complete with protective spells.

During the time of Roman rule in Egypt around the first centuries AD, many mummies were completed by the addition of a portrait of the deceased added to the head area of the wrapped body. The portraits were painted on wooden panels and allow one an unprecedented glimpse into the faces of individuals from this era.

Yes, for Nebseni it is coffins and more coffins to come. And even at an hour when most workers might begin to think about finishing for the day, he planned to stay open. He would normally send his helpers to the wood pile with a list of several names, wood-types and sizes. But today he offers his workers a surprise: 'Go home to your families,' he orders, 'we'll have an early start and another busy day tomorrow.'

It is one of the reasons the workers like Nebseni, he knows; he tries not to exhaust those who assist him. And Nebseni knows full well that he would need their help for as long as Egyptians pass on to the Afterlife.

1ST HOUR OF THE NIGHT
(18.00–19.00)

THE BRICK-MAKER WALLOWS

Magir the supervisor approaches the twenty filthy men toiling away in a pit full of mud. 'You are all slow and lazy!' he spits out. 'You will stay here as long as it takes to complete your quota!' Ezer and his good friend Jemer have no love for Magir whatsoever, and nor does anyone else in the brick wallow for that matter. The fact is that the three men had grown up in the same town together, in Shamash-Edom far to the east. Life there had been pretty good until the Egyptian army came to conquer and punish. At the time, Ezer was a successful merchant, Jemer imported wine and Magir made shoes as an assistant to a leather craftsman, and all three were more or less content.

The announcement that Amenhotep was coming again to their region had been met with great fear. The king's father, Thutmose, had made repeated visits and any chance of escaping death and destruction required giving or at least displaying the appearance of cooperation. Precious goods were to be produced on demand and any later attempts at rebellion would be crushed. Those in Shamash-Edom, however, had had enough, and assumed that Thutmose's son would not be able to hold on to the gains his father had made. They were wrong, and the city had been demolished. All its wealth was taken away, as were hundreds of women, children and able-bodied men.

The long caravan heading west would no doubt have looked impressive to an Egyptian eye, Ezer thought at the time, with numerous captured cows, horses and defeated Syrians who with their beards and curious clothes stood out dramatically from their Egyptian subjugators. The march to Egypt was arduous, with the troops showing little concern for their captives. They always fed themselves first and remained strong and healthy enough to chase down and kill escapees. The whole experience was humiliating, with donkeys loaded with some of Ezer's recognizable possessions on a trek to an enemy's land and an unknown future.

Sadly for Ezer, there is no end of need for mud-bricks in Egypt. Millions are produced every year, and could be used to build everything from the simple homes of the average worker living in a village and the villas of the elite, to the great palaces of the ruler and temples to the gods. And there are plenty of storehouses and lots of walls. Even though typically composed of nothing more than mud and sand mixed with straw, the bricks are incredibly versatile and could be created in uniform sizes as needed by using wooden moulds. And there is little fear of running out of raw materials. The river provides mud and water and Egypt's boundless agricultural fields provide the straw that serves as a binder. The sun does the rest. Apart from their obvious utility, the bricks are also used to insulate enclosed buildings, keeping their interiors cooler in the summer and warmer in the winter.

Not surprisingly, as Ezer has found to his cost, brick-making is one of the most taxing of the many strenuous jobs in Egypt. Mixing mud with straw is mind-numbingly repetitive and could be physically demanding. It isn't just the mixing; endless deliveries of straw are required and water has to be regularly provided to keep the mixture pliable and consistent. None of these activities could be considered pleasant. Even though the straw is delivered on the backs of donkeys, it is preceded by the obnoxious tasks of cutting or gathering, and loading, a process that might be repeated dozens of times daily. Providing water, too, could be extremely taxing, especially if the bricks are made at any distance from the river. Even if the water is nearby, it has to be repeatedly carried in large jugs on the

IT'S A DIRTY JOB! BRICK-MAKERS AT WORK

shoulders of some of the sturdier members of the brick crew, and dumped into the mud to be mixed together by vigorous hoeing.

The bricks themselves are formed by packing the muddy mixture into rectangular moulds, which could vary in size depending upon the nature of the construction project. With a finishing swipe of a wet hand across the top, the mould could be pulled up and off to produce a uniform product. The new bricks would be set in rows to dry beneath the Egyptian sun for a few days before being flipped over to ensure that both sides would be consistently solid. Upon completion they could then be collected by others faced with the physically draining job of lifting brick after brick, over and over, all day long, and then transporting the heavy objects to the construction site. Donkeys could be employed as could a yoke across one's shoulders with a balanced load on each side. As ordered, the bricks might be piled up to build a simple wall, or elaborately configured, with mud mixed with sand providing mortar as needed.

On their own, structures of sun-baked mud-brick might appear visually unattractive, yet they were utilized in countless significant constructions, including royal palaces. The bricks could be plastered over and coloured to provide impressively beautiful surfaces.

Upon arriving in Egypt, Ezer had managed to stay together with Jemer and Magir, and they were transported to Thebes where they were immediately consigned to work making bricks under the abusive direction of a low-end Egyptian supervisor. One day ran into the next and the three often chatted about their old lives in Shamash-Edom, wondering what happened to many of their friends and family members whom they hadn't seen since their capture and deportation. Talk of escape and a return home was unrealistic; a foreigner in Egypt was easy to detect, if only by their language, and the obstacles numerous. Occasionally, though, they quietly admitted that the climate in Egypt wasn't too bad much of the time, the food was tolerable, and there wasn't a regular fear of drought or invasion as was the case at home. But they certainly all agreed that they shared no love for their job, nor was their housing particularly good.

Ezer, like most of the unfortunates to have such a job, shares the floor of a small shack with other brick-makers, to which they return exhausted each evening. His daily ration of bread and beer is sufficient to keep his energy up and occasionally a few loaves and jars could be traded for some other commodities. He owns few personal possessions; anything of value had been confiscated back in Shamash-Edom, and not even clothing is much of an issue. Many prefer simple loincloths, which could be stripped off and put aside while the work in the mud ensued.

The majority of ancient Egypt's buildings were made from mud-brick and most have not survived the ages. Mud-brick erodes and disintegrates through time, and exposure to water, particularly during the Nile's annual flooding, is especially disastrous. The end result is that most of the surviving monuments are temples and tombs, stone structures built for eternity. One should be wary, therefore, of gaining the impression that the Egyptians were obsessed with religion and death simply based on the extant buildings.

In the last two months, though, Magir had apparently forgotten his beloved homeland and, due to his enhanced skills in ingratiation, he had been promoted to supervise his own small gang of fifteen workmen. He now commands the brick-makers as if he's the Overseer of Works himself, yet Ezer thought he, too, must be very aware of the consequences that might result if his underlings don't produce the necessary quantity of bricks. He'd probably end up back in the muck with them. 'Hurry up, lazy ones! I'm hungry and I'm tired of looking at you!' he orders as he struts about in a mud-stained kilt.

Ezer is disgusted and bemused; disgusted that his former friend Magir would treat him and Jemer in such a way, and bemused by how he has taken on a kind of new identity. He now insists on being called by the Egyptian name, Paneb, and would occasionally pretend that he couldn't understand the 'foreign' language of the brick-makers under his supervision. His attempts to be Egyptian are pathetic but it is well known that some outsiders who completely conformed and amalgamated themselves into Egyptian society could be accepted and live well, perhaps even rising to trusted roles. The Egyptians don't despise foreigners because of their skin colour or geographical origin: Egyptians consider everyone else as inferior in terms of culture.

Today, Userhet, a powerful Overseer of Works, is touring the brickyards. All the workers have been told of his coming and ordered to become exceptionally animated and dutiful. Ezer notices Magir sweating nervously as Userhet approaches with his entourage to view the production. 'Greetings, oh Overseer,' proclaims Magir obsequiously with his obvious, thick foreign accent, his wooden baton tucked under his arm. 'I am Paneb, and I am pleased to report that, under my supervision, my men produce their expected quota daily.'

'Paneb?' asks Userhet incredulously with a raised eyebrow. Jemer and Ezer have a hard time holding back their laughter. 'Paneb, then. It is very important that we not only have the desired number of bricks, but that they are of high quality. They will be used in expanding the palace of Amenhotep himself,' said Userhet.

'Yes, Overseer. Understood. I compel my men, vile Asiatics that they are, to do more than what is required, under serious threat of punishment if necessary.'

'As one should,' replies Userhet. 'As one should!' The Overseer of Works smiles before moving on to the next group of workmen. 'Nice work, Paneb.'

As soon as Userhet is out of hearing distance, the expected verbal abuse begins. 'Oh, Paneb! Have mercy upon us vile Asiatics!'

'Paneb? Does that mean "bad friend" in Egyptian?'

'We liked you better when you were called Magir!'

'For an Egyptian, you surely speak our vile Asiatic language quite fluently. Why are you not a scribe?'

'Twenty years a family friend, five years a fellow worker, and only two weeks to become a stranger.' It is Ezer who utters this final taunt.

Magir would not have it. 'Say what you will. I will be supervising a hundred men not long from now and all of you will probably die making bricks.' The supervisor turns to walk away to take his seat on a brick bench nearby.

For many centuries and into modern times, the remains of ancient collapsed and decayed mud-brick walls and buildings have served as a ready source of fertilizer for Egyptian farmers. This practice, now banned, has left archaeologists with even less of the already scarce surviving evidence of Egyptian daily life. While some evidence was lost to this practice, the excavated garbage dumps from the remains of ancient towns have in their turn yielded a huge trove of discarded papyrus documents from the time of the Greeks, Romans and beyond.

Ezer could stand it no longer. Grabbing a healthy handful of mud mixed with straw, he heaves it at Magir's back where it splatters into a sloppy mess on his kilt. Spinning around in anger, the supervisor demands to know who is responsible. It isn't hard to narrow down the possibilities. 'I suspect it was one of you two,' he screams at Ezer and Jemer. Neither say a word. 'Both of you, turn around now,' orders Magir gruffly.

The two do as ordered and brace themselves for the expected crack of the staff across their calves. Instead, each feels a sharp shove against their back, which launches them face-first into the mud. The two emerge from the muck looking like twin creatures, with Ezer only distinguishable by his height. Several of the other workmen laugh until Magir counters with, 'You may join them if you wish! No one is going home until we've reached the quota. None of you! We will stay as late as it takes.' The workers have all heard this before and manage to find grim satisfaction in the fact that Magir wouldn't be able to go home either.

Ezer lifts up a newly formed brick, fresh from its mould, but as he raises his arm to throw it at Magir, it falls apart in his hand, having not yet been baked by the sun. It all seems so futile but, in a few hours, the work would be done, finished in the night by torchlight, and Ezer would go down to the river to bathe, to wash off his body, encrusted with mud from head to toe, so as to be once again recognizable to start a new shift.

2ND HOUR OF THE NIGHT
(19.00–20.00)

THE LADY OF THE HOUSE PREPARES FOR A PARTY

If you are wealthy, and set up a household, be gracious to your wife according to what is fair. Feed and clothe her well … Make her happy all the days of your life.

The Maxims of Ptahhotep

The sun would soon be setting and, although most everything seems in order, Nefret is nervous. Her stepson is to be married and the accompanying celebration is both expensive and elaborate. As the wife of a senior bureaucrat, the overseer Userhet, the best would be expected and there would be many guests visiting their villa that evening. The food would be plentiful including roast duck and beef, and there would be plenty of good wine, some imported. The biggest worry is Userhet himself, who over the years has become a bit spoiled and effete, much to Nefret's embarrassment. Too much wine, frivolity and young dancing girls and her husband could become foolishly jolly and occasionally belligerent; the planned evening's celebration would provide the perfect combination of factors for both.

The two married five years previously and Nefret is Userhet's second wife. His first had borne him only one offspring, a son, and then died in childbirth while attempting to deliver the second. Userhet is now well over forty years old while Nefret is barely twenty and the couple have already produced two children. Her father, a prominent scribe, had encouraged her to marry his friend, the overseer, despite his bad habits, desiring to extend his own family network among the elite. And although Userhet already had a son, he had been looking for a new wife who would be loyal, tolerant and most importantly, fertile.

With the exception of the royal family, most Egyptian marriages were probably monogamous and incestuous couples uncommon. Although one might have multiple wives, it was usually one at a time, and the boundary for marrying one's relatives usually did not step any closer than a cousin. The common practice of calling one's wife his 'sister' was more of a term of endearment than necessarily a genetic reality. The ruler of Egypt, however, might have a chief royal wife, secondary wives, foreign wives resulting from political alliances, and a concubine. Marriages between royal step-siblings, brothers/sisters and father/daughter are known to have occurred on occasion, thus keeping power and wealth within the family.

← →

The act of marriage, as was common, was simply an agreement between the couple, the new wife moving in with her partner, bringing her personal assets to join her husband to form a new household. Apart from some very expensive furniture brought into the home with the joining of the two, Nefret also owns several very productive fields, which are tended by contracted farmers who are allowed to work there in exchange for some of the produce. This property, combined with that already owned by Userhet, made the couple quite wealthy and their home and lifestyle reflect this.

← →

The collection of advice known as the *Maxims of Ptahhotep* provides a guide to etiquette presented in the form of an elderly father of the elite class sharing insights to his son. There are comments about responsibility, leadership and how to deal with people of different status. The several comments regarding women are interesting, including this bit of advice regarding one's wife: 'Do not condemn her, but keep her well away from power. Control her, because her eyes are quick and sharp. Watch her, and she will remain long in your house. If you are too strict, there will be tears. She provides wifely favours in return for her maintenance, and what she asks is that her own desires be fulfilled.'

Userhet and Nefret live in a splendid villa surrounded by walls forming a private compound. Upon entering its front gate, one encounters a lovely pool surrounded by well-tended trees and other plants. The home itself is certainly large and is composed of several spacious rooms perfect for entertaining, and a number of smaller ones for sleeping and storage. The ceiling is supported by attractive wooden columns and windows situated high up the walls allow for illumination during daylight hours. There are several beautifully constructed chairs here and there, and a couple of tables that indicate to guests that they are in the presence of wealth. Nefret knows Userhet very much wants to give the impression of a miniature version of the ruler's own Theban palace, a place he has visited on many an occasion.

Outside in the compound are several adjacent structures including a facility for making bread and beer, and areas for preparing other food. There is a large granary and rooms for storing beer and wine. One of the couple's fields is directly behind the compound so fresh vegetables are readily available, and a small herd of cattle is tended nearby. One of the cows met his end earlier that day and is being prepared for roasting. A number of servants attend to the tasks outdoors, but there are also several indoors, mostly doting on Nefret. They assist her with just about everything personal, including bathing and dressing, and also literally putting food on the table. Nefret prefers older women working in the house as she is well aware of her husband's reputation.

The servants are very helpful in looking after Nefret's two daughters, they being two and four years old. The youngest is tended by a wet-nurse while the oldest spends much of her time playing with her dolls and a pet cat. They are lucky. Even at an early age, most of the working-class children of Egypt would already be assisting their parents at home, or in fields or workshops. Nefret is glad that Userhet's son is getting married and moving out of the house. He is two years older than her and their relationship feels awkward.

A number of toys from ancient Egypt have survived. There are simple dolls, for example, in the shape of a wooden paddle with some braided hair glued to the top, while other dolls are nicely carved with movable limbs. Balls seemed to be popular with their ability to serve in any number of games. The activities of older children often tended to be more athletic, however, including wrestling and acrobatics.

Nefret's tolerance of her husband is the price she pays for their extravagant lifestyle. She, too, had been brought up well and is accustomed to luxuries. Her habit of barking out orders to the servants is well honed from her father's home. Still, she wonders if she could have done better than old, bald Userhet. Why couldn't her father have picked someone less obnoxious? There is always the possibility of a divorce someday. It is almost as simple as marriage but with an agreement to separate and move out. Although she would retain some of her property and perhaps some of his, it would be uncomfortable, and there would be no guarantee that she would be able to match the standard of living she now enjoyed unless she was able to find another single, wealthy bureaucrat who wouldn't mind a new wife and a couple of children.

With the festivities to begin in less than two hours, Nefret makes her rounds. Everything has to be perfect, a fact she has made known to all including the servant in charge of cleaning. No detail would be left unattended. She orders furniture be moved to accommodate the musicians and dancers, chairs set up along the wall and tables, which will soon be covered with delectable food, to be strategically positioned. They would need dozens of drinking cups, and amphorae of imported wine placed in a room off to the side where a servant could readily provide refills. There would be perfumed waxed cones and lotus flowers freshly picked from the villa's pond to present to the guests. The smell of incense mixed with freshly cooked beef would drift over the proceedings.

Confident now that many of the celebration's details are under control, Nefret needs to concentrate on herself. Calling to her trusted personal servant, Iput, she retires to a chamber adjacent to her bedroom and disrobes. Iput soon appears with a couple of young women each carrying a large jar of fresh water. Nefret lifts her arms high as the water is poured over her head, followed by Iput scrubbing her down with wads of linen. Next comes the dreaded part. All trace of hair below the neck would be eliminated. With the help of a sharp copper razor lubricated by oil and a pair of tweezers, the job is accomplished in relatively short order.

Afterwards, Nefret's entire body is rubbed with perfumed oil before she takes her place in front of a small table bearing a hand mirror and an ivory comb. Viewing her reflection in the mirror of polished bronze, she combs her short, wet hair straight. She doesn't need to do much more with it as an elaborate wig would be worn that evening, its beautiful ringlets dropping to her shoulders and secured with a colourful headband. It would be installed and adjusted not long before guests were to arrive. Next, her eyes and eyebrows are enhanced with kohl – dark green today – and then her lips accentuated with a mixture of red ochre and fat.

A BEAUTIFULLY ADORNED LADY OF THE HOUSE COMPLETE WITH JEWELLERY

Nefret is pleased with the results as she continues to fixate on her reflection in the mirror. Yes, she admits, she looks good, hopefully better than the others, and that is the desired effect as the mistress of her own house. There is still much more to do, including the matter of clothing. Nefret has several chests full of lovely garments but tonight she is going to wear a new, beautiful, pleated dress made of the finest, whitest linen. The best weaver in Thebes had finished it just that morning. Nefret was excited when the garment arrived a few hours previously. It is simple: a large rectangular sheet of cloth, fringed on the edges, which is wrapped a couple of times around the body and then over one's shoulder and secured in front. No doubt there would be others at the celebration wearing similar outfits, but the accompanying jewellery is what will make the difference.

Nefret asks Iput to retrieve the special boxes. Inside is a small treasure trove of some of her favourite possessions and, with her selection already decided days before, she opens one of the boxes and removes a lovely beaded collar, which Iput holds in front of her to admire in the mirror. The collar consists of rows and rows of small blue cylindrical faience beads, interspersed by others made of red carnelian and coloured glass. Dangling around the edges are golden pendants resembling teardrops. It is vibrant and suitably expensive, and just the right complement to a bright white dress.

The collar is placed carefully on a table and Iput opens and presents the other boxes. There is a pair of golden bracelets and some elaborate earrings, which are also set aside. 'I'll be the most beautiful woman at the party, won't I, Iput?' asks Nefret.

'Of course you will,' comes the automatic answer. 'There will be many lovely ladies, but no one will compare to Nefret, wife of the overseer Userhet.'

'Must she have complimented me with reference to that annoying husband of mine?' thinks Nefret. 'And I bet he'll be wearing a wig tonight, too, whenever he shows up!'

With clothing and accoutrements laid out to be donned just before the celebration, Iput helps Nefret wrap a simple dress around her body. It is time to once again make the rounds, inspect and give orders.

3RD HOUR OF THE NIGHT
(20.00–21.00)

THE JEWELLER WORKS
WITH GOLD

It is already the third hour of the night but thankfully the gold has eventually arrived. Without it, there would have been a day's delay in the special project: a set of beautiful jewellery for Tiaa, the Great Royal Wife herself. The vizier, Amenemopet, had ordered the set as a consolation gift on behalf of Tiaa's husband, the ruler Amenhotep. The vizier is a loyal friend and advisor to the king and at the slightest hint of marital conflict between the royal couple, he would turn to his favourite artisan, Puyemre, to create something special for his king. Word of the commission had made it down to the jeweller by way of the Master of Goldsmiths, who had sent a messenger to the workshop. This time there would be a lovely and colourful collar, and pairs of earrings, bracelets and armbands, and gold would be utilized in all.

Everyone loves gold, thinks Puyemre. It's bright and shiny like the sun and sufficiently hard-won that it really has special value. It is a sign of wealth and status to be admired – if not coveted. Even some dead people wear it, hoping to enjoy it in the Afterlife, much to the delight of tomb robbers. And for specialty craftsmen like Puyemre, sitting in a chair in the jewellers' workshop, it is malleable and easy to incorporate into nearly any product. It could be melted into moulds or hammered into shape, or applied in very thin sheets to wood, and it always looks opulent. The storehouses of the temples and the palace accumulate large amounts and would dole it out as the need arose.

The Egyptians referred to gold as 'the flesh of the gods' and silver as the 'bones of the gods'. The latter was rare and not naturally available in Egypt and, as a result, it had to be imported from elsewhere, as did electrum, a naturally occurring alloy of silver and gold. Apart from gold, copper was also extensively mined. A combination of the copper and imported tin produced bronze, which could be effectively used in tools and weapons, and in personal items such as mirrors. Iron was rare and mostly derived from randomly encountered meteorites.

Although Egypt has its own source of gold, it typically requires great effort to find. There are mines out in the harsh eastern desert, a punishing place suitable for the foreign captives and criminals who are often sent out to do the difficult task. When a vein of gold is found, it is followed, often by constructing tunnels in the rock. The work is dangerous and exhausting, as blocks of stone are extracted from beneath the surface and removed outside to be further broken up into smaller chunks. These lumps are then pounded into smaller gravel and pulverized. It is all done by hand and, like quarry work, it involves pounding and grinding all day long. With the gold-bearing material crushed nearly to sand, it is washed on a sloping board to separate the gold from the stone. From there it could be bagged and sent under guard to the Nile Valley.

Mining is certainly tough but, as Puyemre knows, the king has other sources of the precious metal. It is seemingly plentiful in the land of Kemet's southern neighbour, Nubia. The Nubians, too, enjoy their gold and the Egyptians could trade for it or, better yet, take it from them through warfare or tribute. The same applies to the lands of the east under Egyptian dominion. Nearly every city or town, it seems, is expected to make forced contributions, often in the form of personal jewellery, to be delivered at a time and of a quantity demanded by their oppressors. It is one of the rewards of building an empire. On the other hand, gold has become a major ingredient of the diplomatic gift exchange with other kings demanding it from Egypt as proof of good relations. Puyemre is therefore all too aware just how valuable is the metal with which he so loves to work.

In 1922, when English archaeologist Howard Carter took his first peek into the tomb of Tutankhamun, he is noted as having said, 'Gold! Everywhere the glint of gold!' Indeed, the virtually intact tomb of the New Kingdom ruler, Tutankhamun, contained a vast amount of gold and gold-gilded objects including furniture, chariots and numerous funerary objects. The innermost of his three nesting coffins was of solid gold, weighing around 110 kg.

As Puyemre arranges his tools on a low table, several craftsmen are at work on other projects. Some are pounding sheets of gold ever thinner into foil while others are bending and shaping vessels that will be used for temple rituals. Early that day, representatives from the treasury showed up with a bag of gold dust and a scale. With a scribe carefully making notes, the gold was weighed and allotted; pilfering is not to be tolerated by those who deliver or those who receive.

The dust was taken to a special furnace to be melted into workable ingots and sheets. The furnace would be stoked with wood charcoal kept at the necessary high temperature by using bellows, which would blow in air to increase the heat. Occasionally, the gold delivery would be in the form of a basket of foreign booty with gems to be extracted from the confiscated jewellery and its accompanying gold transformed in the furnace for reuse.

Jewellers hard at work

Within minutes of receiving the assignment for the jewellery, Puyemre had already been creating designs in his head. The armbands would be of pure gold, but sufficiently lightweight so as not to tax the queen. The bracelets, too, would be made to match and all would be hinged for ease of putting on and removing. The items would be enhanced with inlaid alternating rows of beautiful blue turquoise and red carnelian; relatively simple but very elegant. On the inside of each would be carefully engraved the name of the queen and there would be no doubt to whom they belonged.

The earrings, too, would be relatively simple but attractive. They would consist of a coil of gold wire on which inlays of lapis lazuli, malachite and feldspar would be affixed to resemble a rosette. The broad collar, though, would be more elaborate with three double rows of teardrop pendants of turquoise alternating with circular gold beads. Placed below the queen's neck and hung over her shoulders, it would be held in place by a counterbalance in the form of a golden lotus dangling down her back and linked to delicate chains running from each end of the collar.

The dark blue semi-precious stone, lapis lazuli, was rare and prized in ancient Egypt. Often incorporating flecks of gold, it polished up beautifully and was a favourite material in expensive jewellery. Its source was far-off Afghanistan from where it eventually made its way to Egypt, perhaps after being traded through many hands.

Puyemre is proud of his work and actually has even seen it worn, but mostly from a distance. Although he is admired for his skill, there is always some snooty scepticism among the elite for anyone involved in the manufacturing of anything. The occasional commissions requested of individual artisans are always regarded as special and a kind of competition exists between the craftsmen when it comes to the ultimate recipient, dead or alive. Something requested from, or for, a member of the royal family, of course, would be especially prestigious but the vast Egyptian bureaucracy provides most of the opportunities for unique creations.

Puyemre looks over at a couple of his colleagues, busy nearby, their unfinished projects in various stages of completion. One is fashioning a gold ring with a bezel in the form of a scarab beetle. It is for 'a senior overseer of great influence' but he won't reveal who. Puyemre sometimes wonders whether this fellow worker is actually producing something to take home to his own family, made from the various scraps of leftover gold. Another is cutting out very thin strips from a sheet of gold, which the jeweller says are to be formed into caps protecting the fingers and toes of a wealthy deceased man. This would help him to shine like the sun in the darkness of the Underworld. And even though their owner would never see the work – and nor would his family, beneath the layers of linen wrapping – the jeweller appears to be diligently performing his task with great skill.

Puyemre really doesn't like creating jewellery for the dead. It seems such a waste to see his creations used in such a way. He much prefers that the living could enjoy his beautiful output, into which he put so much care. And if he had his way, he wouldn't be involved with anything but the finest materials and that meant gold, silver and the best stones. For this particular commission, Amenemopet had explicitly stated, 'no faience' and 'no glass'. Puyemre is more than happy to oblige.

Faience, or 'glazed composition', is a ceramic-like material of finely ground sand or quartz that can be made into a paste and formed into a wide variety of objects and then fired. It is recognizable by its glassy glazed surface, which is typically in the broad colour spectrums of greens and blues. Faience was relatively inexpensive to produce and could be used in the mass-production of beads and amulets.

JEWELLERS DRILL AND STRING BEADS TO PRODUCE A LOVELY COLLAR

Looking around the workshop, Puyemre really isn't envious of anyone's abilities. As a child, he was involved in some of the lowlier repetitive tasks such as pressing faience into moulds, helping with the furnaces and stringing cheap beads for inexpensive necklaces. His least favourite activity was drilling stone beads of various hardness. There seemed to be an endless demand and many of the possible mistakes were not easy to repair as beads couldn't be re-melted like gold. The supervisors could be ruthless in their criticism but also generous with praise as needed.

Eventually, Puyemre was allowed to work with a goldsmith and his talent for creativity was noticed. From cheap burial amulets to royal requests, it had been a long apprenticeship and now the recognition is satisfying.

Puyemre sits down on a low stool and begins his work. With the gold now available, including a small hammered sheet, he decides to begin with the armbands, which would be simple and relatively easy to produce but elegant. Previous experience with Amenemopet had revealed the vizier's impatience, and now with some of the jewellery actively in production, it will be easy to claim that all is underway and that the results will indeed be fit for a queen.

←――――――――――――――――――――――――――――→

In 1925, an expedition from Harvard University working on the Giza plateau accidentally found an extraordinary tomb. A deep shaft led to a small chamber, much of its floor covered with delicate gold leaf. The evidence indicated that this was the burial of Queen Hetepheres, the mother of Khufu who built the nearby Great Pyramid. The gold had originally been gilded on to the wooden surface of the queen's furniture, but the wood itself had long ago rotted away. In a very painstaking process, the actual golden furniture was reconstructed and included a bed, chairs, a bed canopy and chests, one of the latter containing beautiful silver bracelets. When the sealed alabaster sarcophagus inside was opened with great anticipation, it was found empty, providing a mystery that has yet to be definitively solved.

4TH HOUR OF THE NIGHT
(21.00–22.00)

THE DANCING GIRL ENTERTAINS

While the sun begins to set, Henti and her fellow dancers can see the lights of the villa as they approach from the village road, each clad in long linen tube dresses that soon enough will be discarded in the corner of a banquet room. Earlier in the week, Henti had been tending her hair in front of her home when she was approached by a remarkably bald official, resplendent in a starched linen skirt and grasping a wooden staff that indicated his authority. It was Userhet, the Overseer of Works. Rumours had been circulating that Userhet's son was to become the husband of another official's daughter. They had already moved in together to form a new household and Henti's suspicions were confirmed when Userhet stopped to chat.

'Are you Henti, the dancing girl?' enquired the overseer.

'I am! How may I serve you?'

'I'm having a banquet to celebrate the union of my son, and we require entertainment.'

Henti thought it odd that Userhet himself would make the preparations, but perhaps he wasn't as completely occupied with his profession as one might think.

'I've seen you dance before and we were all quite impressed. Can you bring along a couple of your friends, too?'

'I would be honoured. When?'

'At sunset. Six days from now, at my villa.'

'Good! How would you like us to dress?'

'With as little as possible. Perhaps something with a few beads.' Henti knew what that meant: 'something with *few* beads'. With her hair well dressed and secured with a headband, and her eyes and lips made up, her 'costume' would leave her virtually naked but for a cord around her waist and a few strands of beads dangling in front and in back. In actuality, it wasn't much better than the popular fishnet dress, which was a somewhat more uncomfortable option and concealed not much more.

'We'll be there. Please provide the usual payment.' This would involve banquet leftovers – some chunks of prime meat and perhaps even some small jugs of wine, luxuries not readily affordable for the average worker.

'Be ready to dance with vigour and assist the Lady of the House as needed.' Userhet abruptly ended the conversation and departed to make additional arrangements.

An old story taking place during the time of the great pyramids tells of a depressed ruler who hoped to be cheered up. With that goal in mind, beautiful young ladies wearing fishnet dresses were asked to row back and forth on a lake while the king watched. The boats lost their cadence when a fish pendant worn by one of the rowers fell into the water. A magician came to the rescue, parted the waters, and retrieved the lost item so the entertainment could continue.

By the time the appointed day comes, Henti had contacted her friends Menwi and Nebet. The three of them had performed together at several similar elite events and feel like a team. Although none have yet achieved the ultimate, dancing before the Living Horus, Aakheperure, at least tonight they would do so before one of his appointees. As they reach the villa, the Lady of the House, Nefret, brusquely orders the girls to assist the musicians while many guests arrive dressed in their finest: beautifully pleated bright white linen dresses and skirts, exquisite jewellery and stunning wigs, if not actual hair. 'Dancers … assist the harpists when they arrive, and then we'll start when they're ready.' Userhet is there giving out at least as many orders as his wife, and sporting a shoulder-length wig that is slightly askew and slowly sliding off his naturally smooth pate.

A short time later, Henti greets two elderly, apparently blind men who have appeared at the door, a young child on each arm. Following are a couple of sturdy young men, each carrying a large stringed instrument. Blind harpists are revered and considered the best, and a real sign of an expensive event. 'Blind musicians,' complains the anxious Henti to her friends. 'They're always late. They probably don't even know if it's day or night! Although I heard that one of them is probably faking it. Someone said they saw him repairing his harp.'

PARTY GUESTS ENJOY MUSIC FROM A BLIND HARPIST
ALONG WITH THE ANTICS OF A DANCING GIRL

The harpists are escorted into a large chamber brightly lit by oil lamps on stands, where they are positioned on opposite sides of the room. The other musicians set themselves up in between – some drummers, a few girls with tambourines and clappers, a couple of flautists and several singers. When one of the harpists gives the word, the drummer slaps his instrument rhythmically to gain the attention of the audience; an effective gesture that cues the other musicians to start. The harpists strum their strings and at just the right moment, all join in to produce a loud sound that catches everyone's attention.

This is the cue that Henti and her fellow dancers have been waiting for. They strip off their dresses and dance their way from the sidelines. With their hips swaying, and their costumes leaving very little to the imagination, the three engage in a synchronized, well-rehearsed routine. Arms together, arms apart, to the left, to the right, head down with hair swaying, head up, spin, repeat.

In short order, the audience is clapping. Although the musicians are animated, the dancers are even more so, their barely clad bodies now beginning to gleam from perspiration in the overheated room. Henti always resents that fact. 'They must think sweat is part of my costume!' she often complains. Many of the musicians are as well dressed as the guests, and like the guests, some are given waxy cones of perfume to perch on their heads. The cones would slowly melt in the warming temperatures, releasing beautiful odours. Henti recognizes one of the lutists. It is Sitre, a neighbour with whom she has had a long rivalry. She is dressed in her finest while Henti is virtually naked. Sitre, indeed, is holding back a smirk as she strums her instrument ever more quickly.

The music quietens down a bit when two singers approach. The anticipated love songs would soon begin. The three dancers take a break as the male and female singers stand across from each and begin to alternately sing lines of love poetry back and forth.

'I am your first beloved; I belong to you like a field, which I have caused to flourish with flowers and every sweet plant.'

'There is no one like my beloved and there is none equal to her.
She is the most beautiful of all women.
She is like the star which appears at the beginning of a successful year.
Lovely is her magnificence.
Her complexion is luminous and her eyes brilliant.
Her lips are sweet when they speak, as she does not engage in excessive speech.'

'My heart swiftly flies as I remember my love for you.
It does not allow me to walk normally, but jumps from its place.
It does not allow me to put on a dress, nor wear a shawl.'

Userhet circulates among the guests, praising the performers and offering cups of intoxicating date wine

THREE MUSICIANS ENTERTAIN WITH A FLUTE, A LUTE AND A HARP

poured by an obliging servant. While his wife is distracted, the overseer also offers each of the now-thirsty dancing girls their own cups, which are quickly drunk and refilled. Soon, the vocal performance is over, and it is once again time for the dancers to spring into action, wriggling and spinning ... On more than one occasion over the last couple of years, Henti has seen a colleague plummet into the musicians, which always seems to perturb them, especially the blind harpists who usually offer the harshest of rebukes. Even if they stay on their feet, drunken, awkward dancing girls might receive a vigorous shove out the door, no payment and a bad reputation exacerbated by the village rumour-mill.

To enhance their renown as 'fun' dancers, Henti and her friends often break away from each other to perform 'solos', approaching guests, both male and female, touching them under the chin and looking over their shoulders with suggestive smiles. Henti knows that it was antics such as this that had attracted Userhet's attention and brought about his unusual stroll into the village. Appreciative guests might pull off pieces of their own jewellery and offer them as a gift, or at least, hopefully, provide a reference for a future engagement.

Henti is feeling a bit dizzy from all the spinning and wine, but after the introduction of the married couple, Userhet yells out, 'Would you like more music and dancing?' The guests overwhelmingly applaud in the affirmative and the raucous music resumes. 'Get back out there!' order the household servants, and the three continued, encouraged by Userhet who gives them additional sips from his alabaster goblet.

Within a few minutes, both Menwi and Nebet collapse on the floor and are carried off into a corner. Henti is left, springing and sweating while the music never lets up.

As she wildly spins much too close to the musicians, she notices too late the strategically outstretched foot of Sitre, the lutist, and lurches and falls forward … smack into the strings of one of the blind harpists, knocking both him and his instrument into a pile. 'Get off me, you vile dog!' he shrieks as his fellow musicians rush to help him. Henti is pulled from the tangle as Nefret immediately steps forward. 'Out!' she commands, and Henti is dragged outside by her arms to the gate of the villa compound and tossed into the road. Her two exhausted companions suffer a similar fate, the dust from the road clinging to their sweaty skin as their dresses are thrown at them. A compassionate servant places all three, slumped limply across each other, on the back of a donkey, which brings them back to their village. Even in her drunken state, Henti is aware that she won't be asked to dance again any time soon.

5TH HOUR OF THE NIGHT
(22.00–23.00)

THE PHYSICIAN
SEES A PATIENT

Neferhotep the physician is weary and wishes for nothing more than to shut down for the evening and take a long rest. It had already been a very long and busy day when, sadly for him, a naked boy caked in mud arrived exhausted after a long run to announce that someone was 'injured at the river' and was on his way. No details were given before he quickly dashed off. A boat accident? An unfortunate encounter with one of the Nile's dangerous creatures? He would soon find out.

The life of a village physician is full of variety: skin rashes, broken bones, lacerations or an ill child with a high fever are a few of the typical situations. Just a couple of hours ago, a young woman appeared in his doorway complaining of a severe headache. After examining her and feeling her pulse, he created a soothing ointment from the fried skull of a catfish and applied it directly to her head while reciting a magic spell in an effort to drive away internal demons. 'Come back tomorrow if you're still in pain,' he advised as the patient claimed that she already felt much better. Shortly thereafter, a workman appeared with a fracture of his right upper arm bone. The pain was excruciating for him as Neferhotep felt the break and then pulled and twisted on the arm until the bone sections were realigned. The relief was immediate and the patient was sent away with his arm anointed with grease and honey and then bound with an immobilizing splint to enhance healing. 'Don't work for a few weeks,' was the final advice given.

Occasionally patients come to him with afflictions of no particular consequence, and some are regular visitors. Take Userhet, the Overseer of Works, as an example. During the last few months, he had appeared several times demanding urgent assistance for 'emergencies' including a common bee sting, a 'swollen earlobe', and indigestion after a lavish party at another high official's villa. And one time, Userhet even had the audacity to show up with a pet monkey suffering from an itch. Neferhotep politely declined to help on that occasion and suggested a veterinarian would be best.

Last week, Userhet arrived seeking a cure for his noticeable baldness. There was to be a banquet soon at his house and he asserted that he wanted to look his best. Although Neferhotep justifiably considered this a frivolous request, he nonetheless consulted one of his precious medical papyri and searched for a therapy. After a few minutes, he announced that he had found a treatment that someone or other in the past had proclaimed as effective. The recipe called for a mixture of equal parts of fat from a hippo, a cat, a crocodile, a lion, a snake and an ibex. Neferhotep located the appropriate materials among the many dozens of pottery jars lined up along three of the mud-brick walls of his healing room, which is actually a large single chamber annexed to his own home.

There wasn't much left of the 'lion fat', but there was enough to provide a first treatment. Luckily, he lives in Thebes, where the possibility of obtaining lion residues, or purported ones, is greater than in a lot of places in Egypt. The ruler, Aakheperure himself, has bragged about his ability to hunt such creatures, and these days there are plenty of exotic ingredients coming in from Nubia to the south. The physician stirred up the mixture in an empty jar and had passed it over to Userhet, saying, 'Apply it on to that shiny head of yours three times a day. And leave a basket of grain with my assistant.'

Egyptian medicine made use of an extensive variety of ingredients to be used singly or in combination for various treatments. Through trial and error, the Egyptians discovered the therapeutic effects of some substances, such as honey, which slows infections. Animal products employed included meats and fats, blood (including that of lizards, bats and pigs), excrement from creatures as small as flies, internal organs, milk and even roasted mice. Almost every known plant seemed to have an application, and numerous medicinal recipes featured one kind or another of vegetable, fruit, part of a tree or spices. Mineral and metal products were also employed, including galena and malachite, clay, copper and natron, the salt-like dehydrating agent widely used by embalmers.

Userhet had enthusiastically thanked the physician, and waddled home to his villa, the medicinal jar tucked under his arm, no doubt with fantasies of a full head of hair within a week's time. 'What a waste,' Neferhotep had concluded. The temple priests actually shave their heads in their efforts to appear clean and hairless, thus achieving the effect of Userhet's purported affliction, and there are plenty of hard-working men tending to Egypt's endless green fields with a similar condition and much more pressing priorities in life. Seeking a cure for baldness seems to be a luxury reserved for the most spoiled of the elite, who themselves, ironically, often sport expensive wigs. Such complaints, though annoyingly trivial, are occasionally part of the job, but the payment would be welcome.

Before being a physician permanently established in the vicinity of Thebes, Neferhotep had travelled with the military on foreign expeditions, treating the most appalling of injuries and ailments. Outbreaks of disease in an army camp could evolve into a truly dangerous situation and perhaps even spark a retreat. But the results of face-to-face combat between rival ground troops and chariots would often result in the worst of his cases. Neferhotep had seen and treated devastating head wounds from the crush of a mace, massive lacerations from axes and sickle-like swords, and plenty of deep arrow piercings. His military experience and consultative papyri provided rules for treatment. In some cases, the diagnosis recognized that there was nothing that could be done and many of those who were conscious and dying begged to have their remains returned to their beloved Egypt.

All that is in the past. He now considers himself too old to travel into battle so a domestic practice suits him. His military experience, though, has served him well. With many royal construction projects underway nearby, there seems to be an endless stream of injuries incurred while on the job, including everything from eye afflictions as a result of the chipping away of stone to broken bones from falls. And many of his patients are workers under the supervision of the balding Overseer of Works himself, Userhet.

Fortunately, Neferhotep has some assistance. His young son, Nakht, would follow in his father's footsteps as expected. Nakht spends much of his day in training, learning both the scribal arts and medicinal practice. It would be important for him to be able to read the medicinal texts and perhaps even make his own copies as Neferhotep had done. Nakht, however, is still too young to have developed professional patience. He had cruelly suggested to his father that he should have offered the obnoxious Userhet a jar of reeking cat urine or donkey dung to rub into his knobby scalp.

Although he has had a very busy day, Neferhotep is grateful that the worst he has seen today, apart from the broken arm, was a child with a snake bite. Ordinarily he would redirect such a patient elsewhere as there are specialists for that, but he just couldn't turn away the screaming child and her two hysterical parents, one who was dangling at arm's length the flattened carcass of the offending snake. There are many different kinds of poisonous snakes in Egypt – several with lethal bites – but even in its battered state, the physician was able to recognize its kind and pronounced it essentially harmless. Taking a bit of honey from a jar, Neferhotep massaged it into the tiny fang holes on the child's arm while offering reassuring words. Digging through a wooden box, the physician removed an amulet representing the protective eye of the god Horus and placed it around the child's neck. Her parents were understandably grateful and promised to return on the next day with some sort of gift.

ALONG WITH PHYSICAL TREATMENT, AN EGYPTIAN PHYSICIAN MIGHT
PRESCRIBE CURATIVE OR PROTECTIVE AMULETS WITH VARIOUS POWERS

Apart from general practitioners, there were several specialists in Egyptian medicine including experts in the eye, women's maladies, afflictions of the stomach and other internal organs, and snake and scorpion bites, as well as dentists. Not surprisingly, the ruler of Egypt had his own collection of the best to serve himself and his family.

A ruckus outside the treatment room announces the arrival of the anticipated patient from the river. Four scraggly men rush through the door carrying a woven mat upon which the victim lies, screaming in pain and bleeding profusely from one leg. As the mat is placed on the floor, one of the men explains that the usually careful Ezer, a brick-maker, was bathing at the river's bank in an attempt to remove the thick layers of clay adhering to his body from a very long day's work. It would have been more sensible to use water from a canal or well, but Ezer was hungry and in a hurry and hopped in the river for a quick bath. Within moments, a juvenile crocodile clamped its jaws around the calf of his left leg and Ezer, in his panic, was somehow able to shake loose the creature and stumble on to the bank. His screams alerted his friends who themselves were quite shaken up by the sight of it all.

The bite has left a series of deep, bleeding tooth marks. Neferhotep hates these kinds of wounds involving animal bites and river water; they could be difficult to treat successfully. Ezer, though, is truly lucky to be alive. A larger crocodile would have not only created vastly more traumatic wounds, but likely would have held him underwater until he drowned. The physician kneels to examine the row of punctures in a pattern representing the crocodile's teeth while Ezer's friends hold him down. Neferhotep provides pressure with a wad of linen over the bleeding holes while inspecting the rest of Ezer's body for additional injuries. 'Nakht! Get some meat from the butcher,' orders the physician and watches his son run out the door.

Grabbing a hefty vase by its handles, the physician pours a large cup of wine laced with lotus blossoms and encourages Ezer to sip from it. The concoction would serve as a kind of anaesthetic to calm his thrashing patient. The potion quickly has its effect, and when Nakht arrives with two thin slabs of beef, Neferhotep is ready to expertly bind the meat against the wounds. 'Now what?' asks one of Ezer's friends. 'Take him home to his family but he needs to be brought back here tomorrow for additional treatment. And tell them to offer a few prayers to Sobek, the crocodile god. Let this be a reminder to you all the next time you're feeling dirty and lazy.' Ezer is carried out on the same mat he was carried in on.

The Egyptian physician relied on treatments from the simple to the complex. A cure for indigestion, for example, might involve a pig's tooth crushed into powder and baked into four sweet cakes which were then consumed one a day for four days. A recipe 'to heal diseased toes' was much more complicated and included a poultice made from ingredients such as wax, incense, wormwood, poppy plant, elderberries, various tree resins, olive oil and rainwater.

Neferhotep thinks about what would come next. Tomorrow the meat would be removed, and then honey and grease would be applied and the wounds rebandaged. He checks a couple of jars to make sure there is a sufficient supply of the anticipated ingredients. That is enough for Neferhotep. 'Clean up the mess,' he tells his son gently, 'and I'll see you ready to heal when the sun rises.' The physician walks next door, removes his heavily stained linen kilt and climbs into his bed. Laying his head on his wooden pillow, he quickly falls asleep for a few hours reprieve before another round of daily surprises.

6TH HOUR OF THE NIGHT
(23.00–00.00)

THE NOVICE TOMB
ROBBER SHOWS
RELUCTANCE

As for anyone who enters this tomb unclean, I will grab him by the neck like a duck, and he will be judged for it by the great god.

FROM THE TOMB OF THE OLD KINGDOM OFFICIAL, HARKHUF

Nemwef squats down in the shallow pit and chips away at the plaster with a copper chisel and wooden mallet. He is slow and careful, but too careful for one of his associates, Bebi. 'Get on with it,' he urges, 'or I'll do it myself!' It is a bluff. Nemwef knows that Bebi wouldn't want to get involved in the breaching; that way he could always argue that he never touched the chisel if he was ever caught. 'No one can hear us in this pit and those who might hear will be recipients of the bounty.' Only slightly more encouraged, Nemwef doubles his efforts and soon the top of a wall of stacked stones is revealed. One of the blocks falls inward, producing a dull thud and revealing a dark void behind. His heart races as he is now undeniably involved.

Nemwef and Bebi, along with four others, are robbing a tomb. And this isn't just an ordinary well-endowed tomb of an official, this is the tomb of Queen Meryetamun, wife of the first Amenhotep. She had died at least a hundred years previously and to the best of their knowledge, it has yet to have been visited by any previous thieves; an exciting prospect indeed. Although involved in theft at various levels since a child, Nemwef is new to tomb-robbing. He had heard that it was going on, but had found the idea unacceptably risky in so many ways, yet the temptation proved overwhelming.

The thieves have plenty to worry about. If captured in the act, or caught with royal burial goods, the penalty would likely be a painful death. And then there is the matter of the gods. Nemwef is now visibly shaking as he is struck with realization. 'Let's stop now before the gods kill us!' he whispers loudly.

'What gods?' responds an exasperated Bebi. 'I've been

doing this now for several years and look at me! I'm alive, in good health, and wealthy! Forget about the gods. If they exist, they really don't seem to care. And as for the queen, she's dead. She doesn't need all of those things in the tomb. What a waste!'

'But they're for the provision of her *ka*!' exclaims Nemwef. 'How will her spirit be sustained?'

'You really believe in that *ka* stuff? Too bad. The fact is, we are alive here and now and we can use these burial items more than a dead queen. And what have the royal family and priests ever done for us other than tax our fields in order to live well, or build tombs for themselves like this?'

'But what about judgement? We'll never survive!'

'Judgement? If the gods ever ask me if I have breached the door of a tomb, I can reply in the negative. As for you, it's too late, you wielded the chisel. Now get to work or leave now. I knew I shouldn't bring you along!'

Tomb curses have become the subject of modern legend, the most famous being that associated with the virtually intact tomb of the late Eighteenth Dynasty ruler, Tutankhamun. Rumours claimed that a tablet was found bearing a threatening curse referring to 'death coming on swift wings' to those who might violate the tomb. Although several visitors to the tomb did die not long afterwards, the fact was that there was no such tablet, and Howard Carter who discovered the tomb in 1922, and therefore was arguably the chief violator lived until 1939. Some intimidating statements have been found on some tombs, but most of them are demands for respect and offerings for the deceased, rather than specifically a curse of imminent death for robbers.

Nemwef picks up his tools and continues until there is enough space for the thieves to climb through and pass out objects from within. 'Let's go in,' commands Bebi, and he crawls through the hole first and lands on a surface on the opposite side. One of the robbers hands him a small oil lamp, which he holds while the others join him inside. Nemwef is last. He hesitates at first with a sick feeling in his stomach but, knowing that he is already deeply involved, he too crawls inside.

The tomb of Meryetamun had been constructed directly under a portion of Hatshepsut's memorial temple. Unlike the high-quality limestone found above, the tomb's corridors and rooms had been carved into an underlying and unreliable layer of shale. It has a strange design with a very short set of stairs behind the sealed door, followed by a corridor and then a right-hand turn into another corridor that terminates by a deep pit, with no way across. The thieves are already aware of this obstacle as Bebi has seen a plan of the tomb provided by a secondary accomplice.

Anticipating the problem, the thieves have brought

a long wooden beam with them in order to span the gap and reach a small hall extending awkwardly off the far left-hand edge of the pit. Given the tight dimensions of the tomb at this point, it is necessary for them to chip away at the floor in a corner diagonally across from the small hall on their side in order for the wood to be positioned. The shale breaks away easily, and soon Bebi is straddling the beam and pushing himself forward to reach the other side. A couple of others take their turn, initially positioning themselves astride the wood so as to be able to pass a few lamps forward.

Everyone quickly and expertly crosses the pit except for Nemwef, who hesitates once more. Most of his larceny has involved granaries, storehouses and a handful of villa bedrooms when the owners were away, and none of which have involved crossing deep pits on a narrow beam. And if he fell in, he is quite confident that his associates would have no hesitation in leaving him there as they went about their looting. He could imagine them unemotionally passing valuable items across the pit as he pleaded for help, and then leaving him to rot or be discovered by the authorities like a trapped rat. Nemwef swallows and pushes himself across the beam to join the others, whom he finds around the corner in a rectangular chamber lined with numerous baskets and jars of various sizes.

Bebi stands to the side holding a lamp while he excitedly shouts out orders, encouraging the search for any portable items of value, especially those things that could be recycled and thus made anonymous so as not to be linked to a burial. A number of the baskets prove disappointing, being filled with dried fruit and other foodstuffs. Nemwef finds others, though, that contain thick, neatly folded sheets of high-quality linen. The inked identifying marks on their edges could easily be clipped off and the cloth likely sold for a very good exchange. Several nicely made wooden boxes are found to contain personal items including cosmetics and mirrors, and there are chests with the queen's personal clothing and numerous exquisite alabaster vessels of various sizes and forms.

A number of small white wooden cases in various shapes lie along the corridor. Bebi says he knows exactly what these are as he gives one of them a swift kick. It bursts open and its contents empty on the floor. It resembles a mummy of sorts, wrapped tightly as it was in linen. 'Anyone hungry for a dried duck?' asks Bebi with a laugh. They, too, were part of the deceased's food provision and are of no interest to the thieves whatsoever. Some of the other cases contain joints of beef or other cuts of meat.

The ransacking continues with baskets being examined or turned over, and a few of the disappointing ones are kept for carrying away some of the desired items. Beyond that chamber lies another, and it is soon clear that this is where the real profit would be made. There lies the wooden coffin of the queen herself, a stunning work of art of enormous size, perhaps twice as big as the occupant herself when alive. For a moment, the robbers gather about quietly, impressed by its extraordinary beauty. The coffin's lid is carved with the likeness of Meryetamun with kind, smooth features gilded in gold, and striking inlaid eyes and brows. Her hands are likewise beautifully represented and most of the coffin is covered with row after row of beautiful inlays. 'What are you looking at?' shouts Bebi to Nemwef. 'Get on with it!'

Some documents describing the trials of tomb robbers have survived from the end of the New Kingdom. The defendants were accused of robbing several royal tombs and several were found guilty. The penalty for such offences could include execution by burning alive or impalement.

The robbers snap out of their temporary daze and without remorse set about their crass work. With experienced hands, several of the robbers use adzes with copper blades to scrape off the gold gilding, collecting the delicate flakes in tightly woven cloth bags. The inlays are removed, too, knocked off or pried out of the surface. Although generally appalled, Nemwef is impressed by their absolute efficiency as he stands by, receiving the desirable items and moving them to the edge of the pit. At one point, Bebi picks up a well-fashioned chair and heaves it against the chamber's wall, where it shatters. It had been manufactured mostly from ebony and its pieces could be recycled. And finding a large wooden box containing four large stone jars, he upends it. The jars contain the queen's mummified entrails. 'Who would like some royal guts?'

Bebi then orders the coffin's heavy lid be removed. 'Let's see if the queen has anything special for us!' Surprisingly, there is another coffin inside, this one of normal human dimensions and also exquisitely executed but lacking gilded surfaces. Nemwef watches a couple of men yank off its cover to reveal a beautifully wrapped mummy. Bebi grabs a knife and sets to work. He clearly knows exactly where to make his cuts. He slices through the wrappings over the wrists and upper arms, and then

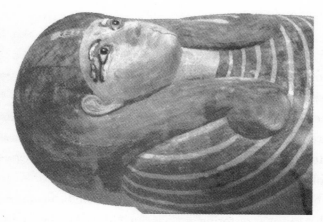

THE INNER COFFIN OF QUEEN MERYETAMUN

The Eighteenth Dynasty tomb of Meryetamun was discovered in 1929 by American archaeologists working for the Metropolitan Museum of Art. It was obvious that it had been violated in ancient times and much of the expected burial provisions were missing. There was evidence, however, that the burial was 'restored' by Twenty-First Dynasty priests hundreds of years later. Noting that the gold foil and inlays of the outer coffin had been removed, the priests had given parts of the coffin a coat of yellow paint instead. Around that same time, additional burials were put into the entrance corridor of the tomb, and thereafter the tomb remained sealed until modern times.

---

moves to the forehead. He is right on all counts and spectacular jewellery is found in each location. He then attacks the hands and feet, finding caps of gold on each finger and toe.

The end result of the carnage is a torn-up bundle of shredded linen exposing the dried-up remnant of a once-living human. 'Take a look at her face,' suggests Bebi. 'Behold, the Queen of Egypt! And nice hair!' he declares, tugging on a few strands of Meryetamun's wavy brown locks. While some laugh, Nemwef refuses to look. His usual thieving never involves violating corpses.

It is time to leave the tomb. There would be no attempt whatsoever at restoring any dignity to the violation, and the queen herself would be left in her pathetic state while the thieves organized their exit. A couple of men are stationed on each side of the pit while two others sit astride the beam to pass the purloined items across. With all back on the near side, bags and baskets are carried through the rest of tomb to the entrance pit from which they entered. Bebi even orders that the beam be brought back with them as it might be useful in future robberies.

Emerging from the tomb, Nemwef is met with a welcome breath of fresh, cool air and a starry sky, the landscape illuminated by a full moon. The job is finished and the goods are divided up for carrying away to a safe place where everything could be sorted out. There are too many baskets and sacks to carry away all at once, but Bebi has anticipated this and has a nearby caching spot where some of the loot can be temporarily hidden. Barely saying a word, the robbers disperse in all directions to meet up later. Nemwef is left with a large basket of linen and told to go away and keep his mouth shut. He hadn't expected much more, it being his first time, and he suspects that he won't be asked along again. That idea doesn't bother him at all; he greatly prefers stealing from grain silos rather than violating the eternal burial places of royalty.

Acknowledgements

Appreciation is extended to my very good friend, the late Barbara Mertz (aka Elizabeth Peters and Barbara Michaels) who epitomized the ability to write engagingly on subjects of the past for a general audience. She is greatly missed. The amazing Dottie Shelton and my mother Patricia Chant Ryan Armstrong, both recently departed, would have liked this book if only because I wrote it. Sherry Ryan and Samuel Ryan are always supportive, as are our feline 'fur-babies', Winny, Nipper and Baby Joseph. The editors of Michael O'Mara Books, including George Maudsley, were helpful and patient, as was Howard Watson. Very special thanks are extended to my excellent friends, Dr Edmund Meltzer and Dr Kenneth Griffin, two brilliant Egyptologists who shared valuable insights and resources. Lastly, many thanks to Lois and Maurice Schwartz as always, and the libraries of Pacific Lutheran University and the University of Puget Sound.

PICTURE CREDITS

Bes (page 17): E. A. W. Budge, *The Gods of the Egyptians*, 1904

Amenhotep II cartouches (page 24): Donald P. Ryan

Amenhotep II engraving at Karnak (page 30): Dennis Forbes, KMT Communications

Scribe Ani's mummy (page 39): E. A. W. Budge, Facsimile of the *Papyrus of Ani*, 1894

Warrior pharaoh (page 52): Adolf Erman, *Life in Ancient Egypt*, 1904

Amun-Re (page 60): E. A. W. Budge, *The Gods of the Egyptians*, 1904

Sacred barque (page 65): Adolf Erman, *Life in Ancient Egypt*, 1904

Farmers (page 70): Norman de Garis Davies, *The Tomb of Nakht*, 1917

Wheat workers (page 80): Norman de Garis Davies, *The Tomb of Nakht*, 1917

Statue (page 89): Adolf Erman, *Life in Ancient Egypt*, 1904

Skiff building (page 102): Norman de Garis Davies, *The Mastaba of Ptahhetep and Akhethetep at Saqqareh*, 1900

Fresh fish (page 106): Norman de Garis Davies, *The Tomb of Nakht*, 1917

Potters (page 112): Adolf Erman, *Life in Ancient Egypt*, 1904

Egyptian script (page 118): Adolf Erman, *Life in Ancient Egypt*, 1904

Hathor (page 131): E.A.W. Budge, *The Gods of the Egyptians*, 1904

Festival drinking (page 133): Adolf Erman, *Life in Ancient Egypt*, 1904

Scribes (page 139): Adolf Erman, *Life in Ancient Egypt*, 1904

Nubians, Libyans and Asiatics (page 149): Adapted from: Giovanni Belzoni, Narratives, 1820

Tribute (page 152): Facsimile by Norman de Garis Davies of a scene in the tomb of Rekhmire, in the collection of the Metropolitan Museum of Art, New York

Tiaa (page 162): Dennis Forbes, KMT Communications

Professional mourners (page 171): E. A. W. Budge, *The Book of the Dead: Facsimiles of the Papyri of Hunefer, Anhai, Kerasher and Netchemet*, 1899

Amenhotep's tomb (page 180): Dennis Forbes, KMT Communications

Valley of the Kings (page 188): Donald P. Ryan

Carpenter (page 193): Facsimile by Norman de Garis Davies of a scene in the tomb of Rekhmire, in the collection of the Metropolitan Museum of Art, New York

Coffin makers (page 196): Adolf Erman, *Life in Ancient Egypt*, 1904

Brick-makers (page 203): Facsimile by Norman de Garis Davies of a scene in the tomb of Rekhmire, in the collection of the Metropolitan Museum of Art, New York

Lady of the house (page 217): Norman de Garis Davies, *The Tomb of Nakht*, 1917

Jewellers (page 224): Norman de Garis Davies, *The Tomb of Two Officials*, 1923

Bead stringers (page 227): Facsimile by Norman de Garis Davies of a scene in the tomb of Rekhmire, in the collection of the Metropolitan Museum of Art, New York

Party (page 233): Norman de Garis Davies, *The Tomb of Nakht*, 1917

Musicians (page 236): Norman de Garis Davies, *The Tomb of Nakht*, 1917

Amulets (page 245): Donald P. Ryan

Meryetamun (page 256): Donald P. Ryan

BIBLIOGRAPHY

KEY TEXTS CONSULTED BY THE AUTHOR

Andrews, C. *Ancient Egyptian Jewellery* 1997

Bierbrier, M. *The Tomb Builders of the Pharaohs* 1993

Breasted, J. H. *Ancient Records of Egypt* 1907

Dodson, A. and Hilton, D. *The Complete Royal Families of Ancient Egypt* 2004

Forbes, D. C. *Imperial Lives: Illustrated Biographies of Significant New Kingdom Egyptians* 2005

Hall, A. *Egyptian Textiles* 1986

Hodel-Hoenes, S. *Life and Death in Ancient Egypt: Scenes from Private Tombs in New Kingdom Thebes* 2000

Hope, C. *Egyptian Pottery* 1987

Houlihan, P. *The Animal World of the Pharaohs* 1997

Ikram, S. and Dodson, A. *The Mummy in Ancient Egypt* 1998

Ikram, S. and Dodson, A. *The Tomb in Ancient Egypt* 2008

Janssen, R. and J. *Growing Up and Getting Old in Ancient Egypt* 2007

Killen, G. *Egyptian Woodworking and Furniture* 1994

Lichtheim, M. *Ancient Egyptian Literature* 2006

Manniche, L. *City of the Dead* 1987

Manniche, L. *Music and Musicians in Ancient Egypt* 1991

Nunn, J. *Ancient Egyptian Medicine*, University of Oklahoma 1996

Peck, W. H. *The Material World of Ancient Egypt* 2013

Quirke, S. *Ancient Egyptian Religion* 1993

Redford, D. (ed.) *The Oxford Encyclopedia of Ancient Egypt* 2001

Reeves, C. N. and Wilkinson, R. *The Complete Valley of the Kings* 1996

Robins, G. *Women in Ancient Egypt* 1993

Robins, G. *The Art of Ancient Egypt* 2008

Sauneron, S. *The Priests of Ancient Egypt* 2000

Scheele, B. *Egyptian Metalworking and Tools* 1989

Shaw, I. (ed.) *The Oxford History of Ancient Egypt* 2004

Simpson, W. K. et al. (eds) *The Literature of Ancient Egypt: An Anthology of Stories, Instructions, and Poetry* 2003

Taylor, J. *Death and the Afterlife in Ancient Egypt* 2001

Tyldesley, J. *Daughters of Isis: Women of Ancient Egypt* 1995

Tyldesley, J. *The Complete Queens of Egypt: From Early Dynastic Times to the Death of Cleopatra* 2006

Wilkinson, R. *The Complete Temples of Ancient Egypt* 2000

Wilson, H. *Egyptian Food and Drink* 1988

RECOMMENDED FURTHER READING

Clayton, P. *Chronicle of the Pharaohs* 2006

Dodson, A. *Monarchs of the Nile* 2016

James, T. G. H. *Pharaoh's People* 1994

Mertz, B. *Temples, Tombs and Hieroglyphs: A Popular History of Ancient Egypt* 2007

Mertz, B. *Red Land, Black Land: Daily Life in Ancient Egypt* 2008

Reeves, C. N. *Ancient Egypt: The Great Discoveries* 2000

Ryan, D. P. *Ancient Egypt on Five Deben a Day* 2010

Spencer, A. J. *The British Museum Book of Ancient Egypt* 2007

Tyldesley, J. *The Penguin Book of Myths and Legends of Ancient Egypt* 2012

Wilkinson, R. H. *The Complete Gods and Goddesses of Ancient Egypt* 2003

INDEX

CHARACTERS INVENTED BY THE AUTHOR